How to Win Friends and Influence People in the Digital Age

Also by Dale Carnegie

How to Win Friends and Influence People

Public Speaking and Influencing Men in Business

How to Stop Worrying and Start Living

Lincoln the Unknown

The Quick and Easy Way to Effective Speaking

Pathways to Success

Also by Dale Carnegie Training

Leadership Mastery

The 5 Essential People Skills

Also by Dale Carnegie & Associates

The Sales Advantage

How to Win Friends and Influence People for Teenage Girls (Presented by Donna Dale Carnegie)

How to Win Friends and Influence People in the Digital Age

Dale Carnegie & Associates, Inc.

with Brent Cole

**SIMON &
SCHUSTER**

London · New York · Sydney · Toronto · New Delhi

A CBS COMPANY

First published in Great Britain by Simon & Schuster UK Ltd, 2011
A CBS COMPANY

1 3 5 7 9 10 8 6 4 2

Simon & Schuster UK Ltd
1st Floor
222 Gray's Inn Road
London
WC1X 8HB

www.simonandschuster.co.uk

Simon & Schuster Australia, Sydney
Simon & Schuster India, New Delhi

A CIP catalogue for this book is available
from the British Library.

Hardback ISBN: 978-0-85720-727-2
Trade Paperback ISBN: 978-0-85720-728-9

Printed and bound by CPI Group (UK) Ltd, Croydon, CR0 4YY

Contents

Contents

PART THREE

How to Merit and Maintain Others' Trust

PART FOUR

How to Lead Change Without Resistance or Resentment

Why Carnegie's Advice Still Matters

In 1936, Dale Carnegie made a compelling statement to his readers: "Dealing with people is probably the biggest problem you face." This is the foundation of *How to Win Friends and Influence People,* and it is still true today. However, developing strategies for dealing with people is more complex.

Messaging speed is instantaneous. Communication media have multiplied. Networks have expanded beyond borders, industries, and ideologies. Yet rather than making the principles in this book obsolete, these major changes have made Carnegie's principles more relevant than ever. They represent the foundation of every sound strategy, whether you are marketing a brand, apologizing to your spouse, or pitching to investors. And if you don't begin with the right foundation, it is easy to send the wrong message, to offend, or to fall embarrassingly short of your objective. "Precision of communication," insisted American writer James Thurber, "is important, more important than ever, in our era of hair-trigger balances, when a false, or misunderstood, word may create as much disaster as a sudden thoughtless act."[1]

Consider the era of hair-trigger balances in which we live today, more than fifty years after Thurber penned the phrase. The stakes are higher. Amid the amalgam of media, distinction is more difficult. Every word, every nonverbal cue, every silent stare is scrutinized as it has never been before. One wrong move can have far greater implications. Still, every interaction from your first good morning to your last goodnight is an opportunity to win friends and influence others in a positive way. Those who succeed daily lead quite successful lives. But this sort of success comes at a philanthropic price some aren't willing to pay. It is not as simple as being ad-wise or savvy about social media.

"The art of communication is the language of leadership," said the presidential speechwriter James Humes.[2] In other words, people skills that lead to influence have as much to do with the messenger—a leader in some right—as with the medium. This book will show you how and why this is true, just as it has shown more than fifty million readers around the globe, including world leaders, media luminaries, business icons, and bestselling authors. What all come to understand is that there is no such thing as a neutral exchange. You leave someone either a little better or a little worse.[3] The best among us leave others a little better with every nod, every inflection, every interface. This one idea embodied daily has significant results.

It will improve your relationships and expand your influence with others, yes. But it will do so because the daily exercise elicits greater character and compassion from you. Aren't we all moved by altruism?

"You can make more friends in two months by becoming more interested in other people than you can in two years by trying to get people interested in you." Carnegie's assertion remains relevant, albeit counterintuitive, because it reminds us the secret to progress with people is a measure of selflessness swept under the drift of the digital age.

We live in an unprecedented era of self-help and self-promotion. We watch YouTube videos like the Double Rainbow go viral in a matter of weeks and garner the sort of global attention people used to break their backs for years, even decades, to obtain. We witness allegedly leaked sex videos create overnight celebrities. We watch talking heads and political pundits tear down their competition and elevate their ratings. We are daily tempted to believe that the best publicity strategy is a mix of gimmick and parody run through the most virally proficient medium. The temptation is too much for many. But for those who understand the basics of human relations, there is a far better, far more reputable, far more sustainable way to operate.

While self-help and self-promotion are not inherently deficient pursuits, problems always arise when the stream of self-actualization is dammed within us. You are one in seven billion—your progress is not meant for you alone.

The sooner you allow this truth to shape your communication decisions, the sooner you will see that the quickest path to personal or professional growth is not in hyping yourself to others but in sharing yourself with them. No author has presented the path as clearly as Dale Carnegie. Yet perhaps even he could not have imagined how the path to meaningful collaboration would become an autobahn of lasting, lucrative influence today.

More Than Clever Communication

While the hyperfrequency of our interactions has made proficient people skills more advantageous than ever, influential people must be more than savvy communicators.

Communication is simply an outward manifestation of our thoughts, our intentions, and our conclusions about the people around us. "Out of the overflow of the heart the mouth speaks."[4]

These internal drivers are the primary differentiator between today's leader and today's relational leech.

The two highest levels of influence are achieved when (1) people follow you because of what you've done for them and (2) people follow you because of who you are. In other words, the highest levels of influence are reached when generosity and trustworthiness surround your behavior. This is the price of great, sustainable impact, whether two or two million people are involved. Yet it is only when generosity and trust are communicated artfully and authentically that the benefits are mutual.

Because we live in an age when celebrity influence can be borrowed like credit lines and media coverage can be won by squeaky wheels, it is all the more critical that every communication opportunity matter—that every medium you use be filled with messages that build trust, convey gratitude, and add value to the recipients. The one thing that has not changed since Carnegie's time is that there is still a clear distinction between influence that is borrowed (and is difficult to sustain) and influence that is earned (and is as steady as earth's axis). Carnegie was the master of influence that is earned.

Consider a few of his foundational principles—don't criticize, condemn, or complain; talk about others' interests; if you're wrong, admit it; let others save face. Such principles don't make you a clever conversationalist or a resourceful raconteur. They remind you to consider others' needs before you speak. They encourage you to address difficult subjects honestly and graciously. They prod you to become a kinder, humbler manager, spouse, colleague, salesperson, and parent. Ultimately, they challenge you to gain influence in others' lives not through showmanship or manipulation but through a genuine habit of expressing greater respect, empathy, and grace.

Your reward? Rich, enduring friendships. Trustworthy transactions. Compelling leadership. And amid today's mass of me-isms, a very distinguishing trademark.

The original book has been called the bestselling self-help book of all time. From a modern standpoint this is a misnomer. "Self-help" was not a phrase Carnegie used. It was the moniker assigned to the genre created by the blockbuster success of *How to Win Friends*. The irony is that Carnegie would not endorse all of today's self-help advice. He extolled action that sprang from genuine interest in others. He taught principles that flowed from an underlying delight in helping others succeed. Were the book recategorized, *How to Win Friends* would be more appropriately deemed the bestselling soul-help book in the world. For it is the soulish underpinning of the Golden Rule that Carnegie extracted so well.

The principles herein are more than self-help or self-promotion handles. They are soulful strategies for lasting, lucrative progress in your conversations, your collaborations, your company. The implications are significant.

By applying the principles you will not only become a more compelling person with more influence in others' lives; you will fulfill a philanthropic purpose every day. Imagine this effect compounded over the dozens of daily interactions the digital age affords you. Imagine the effect if dozens of people throughout an organization followed suit. Winning friends and influencing people today is no small matter. On the continuum of opportunities, it is your greatest and most constant occasion to make sustainable progress with others. And what success does not begin with relationships?

Starting Soft

The business community tends to patronize soft skills, as Carnegie's principles have been called, as if to conclude they are complementary to hard skills at best. This is backward. A permanent paradigm shift is necessary if you want to make the most of your interactions, let alone this book.

Soft skills such as compassion and empathy drive hard skills such as programming, operations, and design to a rare effectiveness. How? Soft skills link hard skills to operational productivity, organizational synergy, and commercial relevance because all require sound human commitment. Does the hard-skilled manager who sits in lofty obscurity lording over his reports trump the hard-skilled manager who walks among his people, who is known, seen, and respected by his people? While the former might win some success by forcing his hand for a time, his influence is fatally flawed because his power is not bestowed on him by his people. His influence is only a veneer of leverage with a short shelf life.

In his book *Derailed,* corporate psychologist Tim Irwin details the downfall of six high-profile CEOs over the last decade. Every downfall was triggered by the executive's inability to connect with employees on a tangible, meaningful level. In other words, every derailment was the result of a hard skill surplus coupled with a soft skill deficit—corporate savvy minus compelling influence. And such failings are no less our own. Theirs were public, but ours are often as palpable.

We lose the faith of friends, family members, and others when we follow the steps of relational success without feeding the essence of the relationships—the measuring and meeting of human needs.

What makes so many well-meaning people get this wrong?

Perhaps the ethereal nature of soft skills leads us astray. We can lean unilaterally on what is measurable.

Hard skills can be tested, taught, and transferred. Most business books are written with this in mind because we can pinpoint hard skill progress—individually and corporately—with charts, metrics, and reports.

Not so of soft skills. They can be difficult to reduce to steps. They are often messy and only crudely quantifiable through better responses and improved relationships. Yet aren't these the best measurements of all? What good is a list of accomplishments if they have led to relational regress? When any progress is bookended by self-promotion and self-indulgence, it will not last.

On a small scale, do we keep friends whose actions regularly demonstrate the relationship is about them? When we learn a person's behavior has an ulterior motive, he has less influence with us than someone we've met only once. The relationship is doomed unless he confesses and makes a change. Even then, a residue of skepticism will remain.

On a large scale, do we remain loyal to brands that regularly demonstrate either an inability or an unwillingness to embrace our needs and desires? Gone are the days when the majority of companies tell consumers what they need. We live in a day when consumers hold the majority on design, manufacturing, and marketing decisions. "Going green" was once a small, well-meaning ad campaign for a handful of products. The collective consumer voice has made it a mandatory marketing mantra.

Individuals and companies insensitive to soft skill success miss the mark today.

Some insist you can't teach soft skill instincts. It is true if you approach soft skills with a hard skill methodology. Carnegie didn't make this mistake. He discovered that altruistic instincts rise to the surface not from shrewd step-by-step strategy but from the exercising of core desires. When we behave in ways that befriend and positively influence others, we tap a deeper well of inspiration, meaning, and resourcefulness.

Hardwired into all of us is the desire for honest communication—to understand and be understood. Beyond that, for authentic connection—to be known, accepted, and valued. Beyond that still, for successful collaboration—to work together toward meaningful achievement be it commercial success, corporate victory, or relational longevity. The crowning essence of success lies along a spectrum between authentic human connection (winning friends) and meaningful, progressive impact (influencing people). "There is no hope of joy," concluded the French aviator and writer Antoine de Saint-Exupéry, "except in human relations."[5]

How does one access these soulful skills that power effective communication, meaningful connection, and progressive collaboration?

We must first remember that today's relational successes are not measured on the scale of media—which ones to use and how many friends, fans, or followers one can accumulate. They are measured on the scale of meaning. Become meaningful in your interactions and the path to success in any endeavor is simpler and far more sustainable. The reason? People notice. People remember. People are moved when their interactions with you always leave them a little better.

Meaning rules the effectiveness of every medium. Once you have something meaningful to offer, you can then choose the most proficient media for your endeavor. However, when you put the medium before the meaning, your message is in danger of becoming, in the words of Shakespeare's Macbeth, "a tale, told by an idiot, full of sound and fury, signifying nothing."[6] The advent of tweets and status updates, while providing convenient ways to keep friends, family, and colleagues in the loop, have created an onslaught of such sound and fury. But it is not only the messages going out at 140 characters or less that are at risk of signifying nothing. Any medium carrying a message that lacks meaning will fall short of its intention: a television ad, a department memo, a client email, a birthday card.

With so few media in his day, Carnegie didn't need to thoroughly address both sides of this equation. He could focus on how to be meaningful in person, on the phone, and in letters. Today, we must thoroughly consider both the meanings and the media of our messages.

Straightforward Advice for Succeeding with People Today

"Simple truths," wrote the French essayist Vauvenargues, "are a relief from grand speculations."[7] The reason *How to Win Friends and Influence People* remains a top seller to this day, moving more than 250,000 units in the United States alone in 2010, is that the principles within it are simple yet timeless. The underlying wisdom is straightforward yet transcendent. Since the inception of Carnegie's first course on the subject in 1912, his simple truths have illuminated the most effective ways to become a person others look to for opinions, advice, and leadership.

If there is therefore any opportunity in rewriting the classic tome, it is not in the context of supplanting its advice. The prose threaded through the pages before you is in a different context: reframing Carnegie's advice for a wholly different era—the same timeless principles viewed through a modern lens and applied with digital, global mind-set. The opportunities to win friends and influence people today are exponentially greater than they were in Dale Carnegie's time. Yet when you break the opportunities down the numbers matter little because "the entire universe, with one trifling exception, is [still] composed of others."[8]

It is true, writes *50 Self-Help Classics* author Tom Butler-Bowdon of *How to Win Friends,* that "there is a strange inconsistency between the brazenness of the title and much of what is actually in the book."[9] View this book's title through today's skeptical lens and you might miss its magic. The book is above all a treatise on applying the unmatched combination of authentic empathy, strategic connection, and generous leadership.

It is important to remember that in Carnegie's time the many media of veneered identities (websites, Facebook, LinkedIn, Twitter) and gimmick-laden persuasion (pop-up ads, celebrity endorsements, televangelism) were not around. The idea of winning friends had not been reduced to an "accept" button. The idea of influencing people did not include the baggage of a half century's worth of inflated ad campaigns, corporate deception, and double-living luminaries. Carnegie had an intuitive reason for identifying his title the way he did.

Back then, if you didn't foster a friendship, influencing a person was nearly impossible. Social media didn't exist. Digital connections were not available. In fact, you rarely did business with a person you did not know in a tangible way. The average person had only three ways to connect with another: face-to-face, by letter, or by telephone. Face-to-face was the expectation. Today it is the exception.

While indirect influence via celebrity or social status existed in Carnegie's time, it was neither instant nor viral like it is today. Friendship was once the bridge to everyday sway. You earned friends with the firm shake of a hand, a warm smile, and an altruistic body of activity. You were worthy of the influence that resulted. The cause and effect are not so tidy today.

Consider the 2010 issue of *Time* magazine's "100 Most Influential People in the World." With more than six million Twitter followers, Lady Gaga made the list.[10] There is no need to discuss whether she has influence over her massive fan base, which has since climbed over 10 million. If she nods to a certain brand of shoes or a certain bottle of water, the products move. The real discussion surrounds the value she ascribes to her relationships and to what end her influence leads. Should she seek the highest measure of both, her influence is a significant force. Should she seek only to increase the numbers, she will make more money but have no more impact than a crack Polaroid campaign.

The inherent, relational value of influence has not changed. It is still the currency of interpersonal progress. Yet the plethora of communication media has made it possible to acquire dime-store versions. And you get what you pay for.

While we live in an era when "noise plus naked equals celebrity," this is not a book about soliciting friendships and exploiting influence, a path Carnegie described as originating "from the teeth out."[11] This is a human relations handbook that originates "from the heart out." It is about winning friends the way your good grandfather won your wise grandmother's heart—through sincere interest, heartfelt empathy, and honest appreciation. And it is about guiding the lasting influence that arises toward mutual progress and benefit.

There is a right and effective way to do this, and Carnegie depicted it superbly. Seventy-five years later, the principles remain true, but some definitions have changed and ramifications have expanded. The trajectory of this book will thus be toward new explanation and application. How do we understand and utilize Carnegie's principles in a digitized world? Certain clues can be derived from lists that didn't exist in Carnegie's time, such as *Forbes* magazine's "World's Most Admired Companies," the *Harvard Business Review*'s "Best-Performing CEOs in the World," and *Time*'s "100 Most Influential People" list, already mentioned. These clues, or at times warnings, have served as occasional guides for the context in which interpersonal success is achieved today. In the spirit of the original book, the pages that follow will also serve as a constant reminder that the reasons we do things are more important than the things we do.

While the journey to applying Carnegie principles today is not as complicated as unplugging and returning to a reliance on telegrams, telephones, and tangible interface, it is also not as trite as injecting a little humanity into every aspect of your digital space. In general, the best practice is a judicious blend of personal touch and digital presence.

Employing this blend begins with an honest assessment of your current situation. From here your path to progress with others is clear.

What is your ratio of face-to-face versus digital interactions? For most people, email, texts, blogs, tweets, and Facebook posts are the primary ways they correspond with others. This presents new hurdles and new opportunities.

By relying so heavily on digital communication, we lose a critical aspect of human interactions: nonverbal cues. When delivering bad news, it is difficult to show compassion and support without putting your hand on another's shoulder. When explaining a new idea, it is difficult to convey the same level of enthusiasm through a phone call as you would if standing before your audience in person. How many times have you sent an email and had the recipient call you to clear the air when the air was already clear?

Emotion is difficult to convey without nonverbal cues. The advent of video communication has knocked down some barriers, but video is only a small fraction of digital communication. And still it does not shepherd the highest standard of human dignity the way a face-to-face meeting can. The award-winning film *Up in the Air* makes this point.

Ryan Bingham (George Clooney) is a corporate downsizer flown around the country to fire people for companies who won't do it themselves. Bingham excels at his job, which requires him to lay people off in a dignified, even inspiring manner. He has mastered a speech in which he encourages each person to embrace the new freedom. He even fights against his boss, who requires him to begin delivering layoffs via videoconference to decrease expenses. The great paradox, however, is that Bingham is a loner without one authentic relationship in his life, not even with his baby sister, whose wedding he may not attend. What appears to be an uncanny ability to empathize and connect with those he is firing is actually a confirmation of profound detachment. It is not until a personal experience shows him the raw significance of real human connection that he finally sees the truth. Then even he cannot follow his advice.

We live in a driven, digital world where the full value of human connection is often traded for transactional proficiency. Many have mastered the ironic art of increasing touch points while simultaneously losing touch. The remedy is found neither in self-preservation (à la Ryan Bingham) nor in stimulating connection through stirring but shallow salesmanship. The former is a philosophical blunder. The latter is a strategic one.

There is a threshold to today's productivity, found at the very point where progress with people is supplanted by progress. Often it's the sheer speed of communication that affects our judgment. Because we believe others expect immediate responses (as we do ourselves), we often don't take the time to craft meaningful responses; we ignore the niceties of common courtesy; we say, "I can't possibly apply these principles to a blog comment, to an email, at a virtual conference where I'm not even sure I can be heard." But these interactions are when Carnegie's principles are most valuable. It is in the common, everyday moments where altruistic actions most clearly stand out.

We expect courtesy on first dates and follow-up meetings; we are impacted when the same courtesy shows up in a weekly progress report or a shared ride in the elevator. We expect humble eloquence in an ad campaign or a wedding speech; we are inspired when the same humble eloquence shows up in an email update or a text reply on a trivial matter. The difference, as they say, is in the details—the often subtle details of your daily interactions.

Why do such details still matter in this digital age? Because "the person who has technical knowledge plus the ability to express ideas, to assume leadership and to arouse enthusiasm among people—that person is headed for higher earning power." It is remarkable how much more relevant Carnegie's words are today.

How to Win Friends and Influence People
in the Digital Age

Part 1

Essentials of Engagement

1

Bury Your Boomerangs

Ask both Adolf Hitler and Martin Luther King Jr. for a basic
definition of influence and you might get similar answers. Observe their biographical application of influence and you will
discover their definitions couldn't be more at odds. The tangible
distinction begins with their words.

Pit "How fortunate for leaders that men do not think" against
"I am not interested in power for power's sake but . . . in power
that is moral, that is right and that is good," and the divergence
is obvious.[1] The former maintains influence is the reward of the
cunning, condescending cynic. The latter maintains influence
is the reward of the trustworthy agent of the common good.
Every day our words place us somewhere between the two
disparate approaches. History details the results at either end. We
communicate toward tearing others down or toward building
others up.

To this end, Carnegie was succinct in his advice: don't criticize, condemn, or complain. But how much more difficult this
seems today. To say we must be more mindful of our words is
an understatement. With an immense digital canvas on which
to communicate our thoughts comes an equally immense canvas

of accountability called public access. "Digital communications have made it possible to reach more people in faster and cheaper ways," explained bestselling *Enchantment* author Guy Kawasaki in a recent interview, "but a loser is still a loser. You could make the case that technology has made it possible to blow one's reputation faster and easier than ever."

It is a good case indeed, and precisely today's counterpoint of applying this principle.

What was once a covert criticism can now get you fined. Ask Dr. Patrick Michael Nesbitt, a former Canadian family practice physician who was fined $40,000 for posting "vicious" and defamatory remarks on Facebook about the mother of his daughter.[2] Or Ryan Babel, the Dutch striker of the Liverpool Football Club, who following a loss to Manchester United tweeted a link to a doctored picture of referee Howard Webb with the comment "And they call him one of the best referees. That's a joke." He was subsequently fined £10,000, about $16,000.[3] Of Babel's tweet, BBC blogger Ben Dirs noted, "Whereas a year ago Babel might have let off steam to his girlfriend, now he has this very convenient—and very tempting—tool at his fingertips that allows him to sound off to the world."[4]

What was once a careless complaint among friends can now get you fired. A 2009 study by Proofpoint revealed that of U.S. companies with a thousand or more employees, 8 percent reported removing someone for their comments on sites such as Facebook and LinkedIn.[5] Getting more specific, a recent online issue of the *Huffington Post* describes thirteen Facebook posts that got people dismissed from their jobs.[6] Included in the list are:

- A waitress at a pizza restaurant who posted her complaint and profane criticism of two customers after receiving a small tip for waiting on their table for three hours, which included staying an hour past her shift. "Thanks for eating at Brixx," she snarked, and then went on to deride the customers, calling them "cheap."[7]

- A game-day employee at the Philadelphia Eagles stadium who posted a derogatory status update in which he condemned the team for allowing beloved safety Brian Dawkins to sign with the Denver Broncos. "Dan is [expletive] devastated about Dawkins signing with Denver . . . Dam Eagles R Retarted!!"[8]
- Seven employees of a Canadian grocery store chain called Farm Boy who created the Facebook group "I got Farm Boy'd" that mocked customers and included "verbal attacks against customers and staff."[9]

At times one can wonder whether criticism has become more prevalent than compassion and judgment more prevalent than grace in our communication media. There is no disputing that snark is chic. With so many opportunities to be heard, many seem keen on thrusting forth their right to speak when someone else is wrong, yet they just as quickly shrink into their right to remain silent when it is they who are wrong. Many are accustomed to holding a sword called the First Amendment in one hand and a shield called the Fifth in the other—all the while forgetting that to do so is to deem human relations a battlefield. In many ways this culture of criticism and complaint is the unfortunate reality.

Yet the influential person understands that such indiscretions quicken the path to relational breakdown no matter how right you are or how wrong the other remains. Such tactics tear down far more often than they build up because they suggest an underlying, unilateral motive whether or not it exists. They subsequently move an interaction from tame to tense. It is no wonder we have more talking heads than true leaders today. Influence is always at stake, but many want nothing more than to state their case. Not only does it set a poor precedent, it does nothing but fuel the tension and increase the gap between a message and meaningful collaboration.

However, when a true leader shows up, there is no disputing the converse effect. There have been few more compelling communicators than the deliverer of the Emancipation Proclamation. President Lincoln was long known as a man who approached tense situations with poise and grace. His reaction to a significant tactical error during a climactic moment of the Civil War is case in point.

The Battle of Gettysburg was fought during the first three days of July 1863. During the night of July 4, General Robert E. Lee began to retreat southward while storm clouds deluged the country with rain. When Lee reached the Potomac with his defeated army, he found a swollen, impassable river in front of him and a victorious Union Army behind him. Lee was trapped. Here was the Union Army's golden opportunity to capture Lee's army and end the war immediately. With a surge of confidence, Lincoln ordered General George Meade not to call a council of war but to attack Lee immediately. The president telegraphed his orders and then sent a special messenger to Meade demanding immediate action.

Meade called a council of war. He hesitated. He procrastinated. He telegraphed all manner of excuses to the president. Finally the Potomac receded and Lee crossed the river and escaped with his forces.

Lincoln was furious. "What does this mean?" he cried to his son Robert. "Great God! What does this mean? We had them within our grasp and had only to stretch forth our hands and they were ours; yet nothing that I could say or do could make the army move. Under the circumstances almost any general could have defeated Lee. If I had gone up there I could have whipped him myself."

In bitter disappointment, a normally restrained Lincoln sat down and wrote Meade what was, given his history, a harsh letter.

My dear General,

I do not believe you appreciate the magnitude of the misfortune involved in Lee's escape. He was within our easy grasp, and to have closed upon him would, in connection with our other late successes, have ended the war. As it is, the war will be prolonged indefinitely. If you could not safely attack Lee last Monday, how can you possibly do so south of the river, when you can take with you very few—no more than two-thirds of the force you then had in hand? It would be unreasonable to expect and I do not expect that you can now affect much. Your golden opportunity is gone, and I am distressed immeasurably because of it.

It was a letter quite justified in being sent. Yet Lincoln never sent it. It was found among his papers after his death.

What do you suppose kept the president from venting his great disappointment and understandable criticism?

President Lincoln was a master communicator, and humility was at the heart of all he said. He must have considered that if he sent the letter, it would have relieved some of his frustration but simultaneously ignited resentment in General Meade, further impairing the man's usefulness as a commander. Lincoln knew Meade had just been assigned to be commander of the Army of the Potomac only days before. He also knew Meade enjoyed a string of heroic successes. Certainly Meade was under a great deal of pressure, with the added burden of bad blood between him and some of those he was being asked to command. Had Lincoln brushed such details aside and sent his letter, he certainly would have won the battle of words, but he would have suffered loss in the war of influence.

This does not mean General Meade did not deserve to be informed of his error. It does mean there was an ineffective way to inform him and an effective way. Lincoln did eventually convey to Meade his disappointment, but he did so in a dignifying manner. In choosing to graciously withhold the more cutting letter, Lincoln chose to retain and even increase his influence with Meade, who would go on to be a force for civic good in his hometown of Philadelphia until his death in 1872.

Lincoln seemed to know, perhaps more than any other American president in history, when to hold his tongue and when silence was a graver mistake than speaking up. At the core of this skill was an understanding of one of the most foundational truths of human nature. We are self-preserving creatures who are instinctively compelled to defend, deflect, and deny all threats to our well-being, not the least of which are threats to our pride.

Consider the steroids scandal in Major League Baseball. Of the list of 129 players linked to steroid and human growth hormone use via positive tests, the Mitchell Report, or implications by colleagues, only sixteen admitted use.[10]

Merely high-profile athletes with high-profile egos?

Not so fast. Consider the last time a colleague came down on you for something you said or did. Are we to suppose his words made you want to give the guy a hug and buy him lunch? Or did you want to hide an open can of sardines in his desk? And that's probably being nice.

Neither you nor I enjoy being the subject of disapproval, whether or not it is deserved. "As much as we thirst for approval," explained endocrinologist Hans Selye, "we dread condemnation."

When we attempt to use criticism to win an argument, to make a point, or to incite change, we are taking two steps backward. People can be led to change as horses can be led to water, but deprecation will rarely inspire the results you are aiming for. We are not merely speaking of public discourse. This is just as true in private conversation.

Despite a zeitgeist of denigrating commentary in blogs, talk shows, and social media, the moment you use a medium to criticize, the subject of your criticism is compelled to defend. And when another is defensive, there is little you can say to break through the barriers he has raised. Everything you say is then filtered through skepticism, or worse, complete incredulity. In this way critical comments act like invisible boomerangs. They return on the thrower's head.

This occurs all the more quickly in a world where nearly everything we communicate is a keystroke, mike, or phone cam away from international exposure. Actor Mel Gibson learned an unfortunate lesson when the profane, racially charged condemnation he left on his ex-girlfriend's voicemail was broadcast to the world. His global influence, once a significant force out of Hollywood, took a huge hit.

A less volatile yet still damaging example occurred in July 2008, when a Fox News microphone picked up comments that, according to a CNN blog post, "the Reverend Jesse Jackson meant to deliver privately that seemed to disparage the presumptive Democratic nominee for appearing to lecture the black community on morality."[11] Despite Jackson's instant public apology, his comments put a dent in his national influence on matters important to members of the black community. Furthermore, they placed into question his support of the Illinois senator Barack Obama, who would soon become the forty-fourth U.S. president.

While most of us will avoid such widely publicized communication gaffes, before we rest in judgment of public figures who have stumbled, we would do ourselves well to consider what others might say should our worst private outburst become public. Better still to always follow a simple principle in our dealings with others—don't criticize, condemn, or complain. We live in an age where the world can hear our words, where global accountability is a very real possibility, where our communication catastrophes can follow us indefinitely.

Despite a global trend toward loose talk, it is neither wise nor necessary to criticize others to make your messages more effective, more important, or more newsworthy. The degree to which you can be heard today is best thought of not as a burden or blessing but as a responsibility. Those who accept this responsibility with humility, compassion, and a trustworthy zeal are much quicker to rise because others remain willing to listen. The people most widely respected within industries, companies, families, and groups of friends are those who are clear in their own viewpoints while remaining compassionate with those whose minds or behavior they would like to influence.

Change by force of words is called coercion in some scenarios. There is a reason it is a crime. And while it might not be illegal between two coworkers, colleagues, or friends, we'd do just as well to avoid any sentiment of it.

The simplest way is to focus on improving yourself instead of others.

- Shift your use of media from a spirit of exposé and objection to a spirit of encouragement and exhortation. There is nothing wrong with informing your friends and fans, even about the things they might want to avoid, but the spirit of your information is key. Are you sharing information because you have an ax to grind? This sort of communication is better reserved for the safety of a trusted colleague's couch. Even if people are already on your side, bragging and whining don't bring them closer. If anything, such behavior makes them question whether they can trust you with their own mistakes and musings.

- Resist badmouthing as a differentiation strategy. Its long-term effect is far more harmful than helpful. In a global economy, you never know when your greatest competitor will become your greatest collaborator. What will you do when the best road to business growth goes through someone with whom you have already burned the relational bridge? Competition is healthy and should be respected. Collaboration is critical and should be protected.

- Make your messages meaningful by removing your agenda. Whether you are tweeting big news to a large fan base or updating a handful of board members, it's wise to remember that no one wants a barrage of what's important to you. Above all, the recipients of every bit and byte of your communication want value. If all you do is fill their ears, inboxes, and iPhones with descriptions of your latest problem or biggest gripe, they won't listen for long. There is enough positive communication available to let another's downbeat dogma fill our minds.

- Calm yourself before communicating to another. When you are put off, the first five minutes are usually the most volatile. If you can train yourself to stuff the knee-jerk response, you will save yourself hours of backpedaling, backscratching, and brownnosing down the road. While we all have our moments of indiscretion, there is little worse than a private indiscretion gone public. Save yourself the small trouble—and potentially extensive dilemma—by taking a step back before spouting something you might come to regret.

While there is always something to say in appraisal of another, it is good to remember that there is always something to be said in appraisal of you, too. The ancient Jewish proverb provides appropriate wisdom here: "For in the way you judge, you will be judged; and by your standard of measure, it will be measured to you."[12]

And while it is difficult at times to downplay our right to speak freely, a quick scan through history will remind you that the greatest influencers are those who held their tongue and swallowed their pride when the tide of negative emotion was arising, and instead let brevity, humility, and wisdom say far more than a critical tirade ever could.

Perhaps there is no more memorable example than the prolific British writer G. K. Chesterton's reply to an invitation by the *Times* to write an essay on the subject "What's Wrong with the World?"

Chesterton's response:

Dear Sirs,
* I am.*
Sincerely,
G. K. Chesterton[13]

It is no surprise that a 1943 *Time* review of his book *Orthodoxy* reported that the robust writer's most popular antagonist, Irish playwright George Bernard Shaw, called him "a man of colossal genius."[14] The same review referred to Shaw as the "friendly enemy" of his contemporary. Even Chesterton himself described the uniquely spirited relationship between the two as that of "cowboys in a silent movie that was never released."[15] The men were at odds on most every issue of their day, yet the spirit of their relationship never was, thanks in large part to Chesterton's ability to keep his ego in check and respect the opinions of a man who couldn't have disagreed with him more. The result was not uncommon in the writer's life.

Chesterton's influence reached well beyond, perpetually engaging the minds of contemporaries such as Bernard Shaw, Oscar Wilde, and H. G. Wells. His book *The Everlasting Man* contributed to the Christian conversion of C. S. Lewis, then an atheist; his biography of Charles Dickens was largely responsible for creating a popular revival and serious scholarly reconsideration of Dickens's work; his novel *The Man Who Was Thursday* inspired the Irish Republican leader Michael Collins with the idea "If you didn't seem to be hiding nobody hunted you out"; and his column in the *Illustrated London News* on September 18, 1909, had a profound effect on Mahatma Gandhi.[16]

To win friends and influence others in today's world takes less than clever rhetoric. It takes the understated eloquence of grace and self-deprecation. If I am the problem with the world, and you are too, then we can stop worrying about who is right and get on with the work of making our world better. Bury your boomerangs and your words will forge a much quicker path to progress.

2

—

Affirm What's Good

The Academy Award–winning film *The King's Speech* tells the story of how a common man with an uncommon touch helped a stuttering prince become a king who would rally a nation.

Prince Albert, Duke of York, had a stammering problem that hindered every part of his life. He had trouble telling stories to his children, trouble communicating in public speeches, and trouble speaking on the radio, the latest technology of the day. In searching out a cure for his ailment, the prince met with an Australian-born speech therapist named Lionel Logue. Logue's methods were unconventional, in no small part because he believed stammering was as much a psychological problem as it was a physical one.

The film shows how the prince, known as Bertie to his family, resists Logue's entreaties, and the rest of the film recounts the rising tension between the men as the stakes are raised and Prince Albert, Duke of York, becomes King George VI, rex imperator, and world war looms.

Finally, in a breakthrough moment as they prepare for his coronation, the soon-to-be king snaps and lets loose with all of his fears—that he will fail his nation and become a laughingstock for all of history.

"Bertie," Logue interjects, "you're the bravest man that I know."

Bertie stops and considers the weight of those words. They portend life-changing impact.

If Emerson was right when he remarked, "The ancestor of every action is a thought," then what Logue had done was that most brilliant of influence strategies.[1] He had introduced a thought that had theretofore never been considered. Bertie, the stammering prince, wasn't weak. He wasn't a loser or a laughingstock. The lifetime of teasing he'd endured and the very picture he had of himself weren't telling the full story. There was something in him that was more fundamentally true, something that was good . . . maybe even great.

Bertie embraced it. And ultimately he would become a different man because one person had the discernment to affirm in him something others had let his shortcomings obscure.[2]

Contrast Logue's actions with those of dismissed NPR executive vice president Ron Schiller, who was caught on video articulating his disparagement of those political parties with which he did not associate. The primary difference between the two approaches is ultimately a matter of choice.

Neither Bertie nor any political party is without its share of faults. It is not as though Lionel Logue had a more righteous subject with which to deal than did Ron Schiller. Both could find reasons to denounce their subjects. Logue simply took the more influential path, the path that held human dignity in the highest regard. Schiller took a path in which he forgot himself and his fellow humans. It isn't difficult to see which path is wiser.

One ancient and powerful Jewish parable involves a shepherd guarding one hundred sheep. They are under his care and he will not let them down. However, at roundup one evening he notices one is gone. Just one. Ninety-nine are safe and secure. What does the shepherd do? Does he say a prayer and hope the sheep shows up before a wolf nabs him? No, he pens the ninety-nine and goes looking. That one sheep is of such magnificent importance the shepherd cannot bear to see him left alone.[3]

Consider the message this sends to the sheep, not just the one but also the other ninety-nine who look to the shepherd for provision and protection. Now consider sending that same message to those you'd like to influence. Have you let them know just how valuable you think they are? There is great power in this simple principle, embodied regularly.

We all have an innate, unquenchable desire to know we are valued, to know we matter. Yet affirming this in each other is among the most challenging things to do in our day and age.

How obsessed we can be with the least important, most superficial things around. Weeks of life spent bantering about some celebrity's latest style or some athlete's latest sin. Hours observing the sociology of a household of clamoring college students. Even if we aren't caught up in the often maniacal musings of pop culture, the demands on our time can still be so intense it seems difficult to dig down deep on anything. When we have a torrent of text messages, email bins that are overflowing, and networks offering ceaseless socializing, even that spouse we courted so passionately can become an inconvenience. Then there are the kids and grandparents and neighbors and so on. Who has time to affirm the good about anything save perhaps a neighbor's new car or kitchen? That's quick and painless.

The problem is that quick and painless can also be mundane and meaningless. It is for these reasons that employing this principle matters so much today.

Affirming the good in others should not however be confused with flattery.

The difference? Genuine concern.

A young, unkempt college student once asked Muhammad Ali what he should do with his life. He could not decide whether to continue his education or go out into the world to seek his fortune. It was clear he was leaning toward the latter. "Stay in college, get the education," advised Ali. "If they can make penicillin out of moldy bread, they can make something out of you!"[4]

Ali was clearly making light of the situation. Ultimately he understood what the kid had likely been told his whole life, and he used a bit of levity to make a significant point: "Don't give up so easily. Stay the course. Despite what you've been told, you matter and you can accomplish something great."

Affirmation, in contrast to flattery, requires seeing someone well enough to sense what to affirm, knowing someone well enough to be aware of what really matters. Flattery is usually an admittance of insensibility, a betrayal of trust. We say things we think we should say, but in reality we aren't thinking at all. What message does flattery send? "You don't matter enough for me to pay you much mind."

We have to overcome the temptation to live on autopilot. Bestselling author Rick Warren writes:

> We rush out the door and say, "Hey, how are you doing? Nice to see you." We don't even look people in the eye. We're not really talking to them. If you do that, you're going to miss a lot of potential in other people. . . . People aren't things to be molded, like clay. That's not your job. That's manipulation—not leadership. People aren't things to be molded; they're lives to be unfolded. And that's what true leaders do. They unfold the lives of others and help them reach their God-given potential.[5]

It is unreasonable to expect any of us to be on our A-game all of the time. Certainly we all miss opportunities we should have taken. But we can all measure our own scales over time. Do the messages you send with your written words, your spoken words, your presence, tip the scales toward affirmation or aloofness? The more they lean toward affirmation, the more influence you will gain with others.

Emerson wrote, "Every man is entitled to be valued for his best moments."[6] Think about that for a moment. Which relationship is most strained in your life right now? What would it look like if you began focusing on that person's best moments and sought to affirm them? This doesn't presuppose the person doesn't have his faults. It doesn't even presume he has fewer faults than fine qualities. He might be a broken man with years of waste and wrongdoing in his wake. But one thing you can be sure of: if you aim to influence him to change, repeatedly pointing out his rap sheet will do you little good. If instead you begin to remind him of what he could be—not with hypothetical hype, but with his own history of goodness, of success, of insight, even if only a brief history—something inside him would have cause to awaken. He could begin to see what he can still be, despite what he has been. "When we treat man as he is, we make him worse than he is; when we treat him as if he already were what he potentially could be, we make him what he should be."[7]

Few in history have understood the power of affirming the good in others better than the sixteenth president of the United States. With this one idea Abraham Lincoln kept the nation together. When he took the oath of office in March 1861 it was far from certain that there would ever be another inaugural address for a U.S. president.

The same day he was sworn in, the Stars and Bars, the Confederacy's new flag, was first raised over Montgomery,

Alabama. In the months since Lincoln had been elected, seven states seceded from the Union. Everyone, friend and foe alike, wanted to know what this man had to say about the breakaway states.

History now views this as one of the greatest speeches ever given, precisely because Lincoln wrote with a spirit of reconciliation. He wasn't weak—he warned about the consequences of any attack on the Union. But he had the vision to affirm what was good at a moment when almost no one else could: "We are not enemies, but friends. We must not be enemies."

———

What audacity this took. Seven states had already broken away and declared independence. War loomed. Friends? How could they possibly be seen as friends?

Consider the last time a coworker betrayed you, a client lied to you, or a vendor failed to deliver on a promise. Was your first reaction to remember what he had done that was still good and true?

Being disappointed, let down, or betrayed are among our most frustrating, maddening moments. Yet they also afford us rare moments to make a supreme impression.

Do you recall a time someone surprised you with undeserved grace or unconditional forgiveness? The occurrence might have taken place many years ago, even during your childhood. Yet the person is likely a permanent part of your memory, with the emotion you felt still tangible.

Ultimately, gaining influence is about setting yourself apart, stepping to a higher plane in the mind and heart of another. If all you do is act and react like anyone would, you will never be set apart. The reasons are simple.

Competition for attention is constant. Communications are often a blur. It is challenging enough to become influential in today's express-lane rat race. You need moments to show yourself altruistic and trustworthy, and seconds are all you are typically afforded. Were we all perfect individuals without a shortcoming in our lives, gaining influence through differentiation would fall solely on your ability to display a greater measure of trustworthiness than the others in a person's sphere of influence. That's a hard line to follow if your competition were all mistake-free individuals like yourself. In this scenario, competing for influence would look more like a beauty pageant (and some still treat it as such).

That's not the case. We are all imperfect beings full of shortcomings, and this affords us perhaps as many opportunities to affirm others after disagreement or disappointment as in the midst of affability. The key is to allow yourself no claim on circumstantial exemptions—use a spirit of affirmation to convey your thoughts about others whenever you can.

Lest you make the mistake some do, a spirit of affirmation despite another's faults is not a show of weakness or passivity. It is not a denial of justice, either, for mercy without justice is meaningless. Lincoln saw beyond the obvious and saw what might happen, and he pursued it.

> Though passion may have strained, it must not break our bonds of affection. The mystic chords of memory, stretching from every battlefield and patriot grave to every living heart and hearthstone all over this broad land, will yet swell the chorus of the Union.

Sometimes affirming the good in others will mean reminding ourselves of that very good that exists in another. Yes, Lincoln said, things are strained, but the bonds of amity are stronger still. There was an American history the South and the North both shared. They'd declared independence together, built a nation together, endured war together, and all needed to be reminded of it: "When again touched, as surely they will be, by the better angels of our nature."

Those final words are the summation of all that needed to be affirmed. There was something bigger than discord hidden deep within, a better and truer reality that needed permission to breathe.

From a British monarch to a divided young nation, an appeal to the good in others turned a tense situation into a compelling challenge to change. This is not, as some might be tempted to think, an action that ignores the problems between you and another. Rather, it addresses them head-on but in a respectful, dignifying manner that is far more successful at propelling another toward repentance, reconciliation, or improvement.

In *You Can't Lead with Your Feet on the Desk,* Ed Fuller, president and managing director at Marriott International, asserts, "No worthwhile business relationship, whether with your own people or customers and partners, can endure without mutual respect. And as I've learned firsthand, showing adversaries that you regard them with admiration can resolve even violent conflicts."

Fuller then tells the story of a brawl that broke out between a Marriott attorney and a hotel owner in South America when the renegotiation of a management agreement escalated into a shouting match, and the two grown men began wrestling in a hotel conference room. The struggle continued without the intervention of bystanders until the hotel owner's revolver hopped out of its holster and bumped across the floor. The wrestlers were immediately pried apart with damaged egos and no resolution.

A few months passed without progress on the matter until

a corporate lawyer and two company executives suggested the Marriott president pay the hotel owner a visit. Fuller describes the events that followed:

> I flew to his hometown and spent two days traveling with him, visiting his businesses, dining at his club, and mingling with his friends. As we got to know each other apart from our business dealings, our mutual respect grew. Seeing him in a different light allowed me to understand the strength of his commitment to his employees, family, and community. The differences at the heart of the conflict weren't resolved, but I realized that he deserved my respect for who he was and what he had accomplished. A week after I left, we reached an agreement with the owner.[8]

Affirming what's good, as with every principle in this book, is not just for grandly titled people at massive moments in human history. It is for this time and this age, where the spirit of communication is often less than dignifying. From the political podium to the digital medium to the boardroom table, the one who speaks in a spirit of respectful, unhyperbolic affirmation will always win more friends and influence more people to positive progress than the one who communicates in criticism, condemnation, and condescension.

The beauty of this principle today is that our affirmation of others is not limited to tangible interface. "While nothing can replace the effectiveness of your face-to-face interactions," explained TOMS Shoes founder Blake Mycoskie in a recent interview, "it's important to remember that the digital world can enhance relationship building."[9] At any moment of our day we can spread messages that affirm our friends, fans, and followers in numerous ways over email, Twitter, text, and blogs.

Don't, however, make the mistake of separating the scalability of a message from the individual significance of the message. They are inextricably linked. As big as a business gets, as large a following as one accumulates, messages are still given and received on an individual level.

What builds a bridge of influence between a king and his speech therapist is the same principle that builds a bridge of influence between a company and its customers or an executive and her reports or a father and his child.

We are all united by one single desire: to be valued by another. Whether this message is conveyed is not a group decision. Each individual to whom a message was directed— whether the individual sits alone across a table or in a crowd of three thousand—determines it.

In Carnegie's original book he offered a story that has, perhaps more than any other story in its pages, struck a chord with millions of readers the world over. It was not his story. It belonged to a man named W. Livingston Larned, who called it "Father Forgets."

Carnegie included it as an encouragement to all of us who can so easily forget ourselves and spend days critiquing and criticizing others. It is included here with a different perspective—not of the father who finally sees his mistakes but of the young son who with an unconditional spirit of affirmation wields a level of influence that changes his father forever.

> Listen, son: I am saying this as you lie asleep, one little paw crumpled under your cheek and the blond curls stickily wet on your damp forehead. I have stolen into your room alone. Just a few minutes ago, as I sat reading my paper in the library, a stifling wave of remorse swept over me. Guiltily I came to your bedside.
>
> These are the things I was thinking, son: I had been cross to

you. I scolded you as you were dressing for school because you gave your face merely a dab with a towel. I took you to task for not cleaning your shoes. I called out angrily when you threw some of your things on the floor.

At breakfast I found fault, too. You spilled things. You gulped down your food. You put your elbows on the table. You spread butter too thick on your bread. And as you started off to play and I made for my train, you turned and waved a hand and called, "Goodbye, Daddy!" and I frowned, and said in reply, "Hold your shoulders back!"

Then it began all over again in the late afternoon. As I came up the road I spied you, down on your knees, playing marbles. There were holes in your stockings. I humiliated you before your boyfriends by marching you ahead of me to the house. Stockings were expensive—and if you had to buy them you would be more careful! Imagine that, son, from a father!

Do you remember, later, when I was reading in the library, how you came in timidly, with a sort of hurt look in your eyes? When I glanced up over my paper, impatient at the interruption, you hesitated at the door. "What is it you want?" I snapped.

You said nothing, but ran across in one tempestuous plunge, and threw your arms around my neck and kissed me, and your small arms tightened with an affection that God had set blooming in your heart and which even neglect could not wither. And then you were gone, pattering up the stairs.

Well, son, it was shortly afterwards that my paper slipped from my hands and a terrible sickening fear came over me. What has habit been doing to me? The habit of finding fault, of reprimanding—this was my reward to you for being a boy. It was not that I did not love you; it was that I expected too much of youth. I was measuring you by the yardstick of my own years.

And there was so much that was good and fine and true in

your character. The little heart of you was as big as the dawn itself over the wide hills. This was shown by your spontaneous impulse to rush in and kiss me good night. Nothing else matters tonight, son. I have come to your bedside in the darkness, and I have knelt there, ashamed!

It is a feeble atonement; I know you would not understand these things if I told them to you during your waking hours. But tomorrow I will be a real daddy! I will chum with you, and suffer when you suffer, and laugh when you laugh. I will bite my tongue when impatient words come. I will keep saying as if it were a ritual: "He is nothing but a boy—a little boy!"

I am afraid I have visualized you as a man. Yet as I see you now, son, crumpled and weary in your cot, I see that you are still a baby. Yesterday you were in your mother's arms, your head on her shoulder. I have asked too much, too much.

Isn't it profound the influence one is afforded—even the smallest among us—when affirmation comes clean off our tongue and clear from our hearts? All great progress and problem solving with others begins when at least one party is willing to place what is already good on the table. From there it is much easier to know where to begin and how to lead the interaction to a mutually beneficial end.

3

—

Connect with Core Desires

In early 2002, *Time* put an odd-looking computer on its cover. It had a small, domed base and a jointed, shiny chrome neck affixed to a flat-screen monitor that enabled it to be pushed, pulled, turned, lowered or raised with the nudge of a finger. It was called the iMac, and the company introducing it, Apple Computer, desperately needed it to work in order to stay in business.[1]

Apple had always been the darling of a particular computing niche—generally creative, antiestablishment types. But in the article that accompanied the cover story, its CEO, Steve Jobs, enunciated a brand-new vision for consumers.

He said he believed the future lay in the PC as the "digital hub" of camcorders, digital cameras, MP3 players, Palm PDAs, cell phones, and DVD players. He risked the company's future on a vision of a place where an entire digital life could be consolidated. And so with the iMac came a free suite of software that today is synonymous with the digital age—iTunes, iPhoto, and iMovie.

Critics and competitors mocked Jobs. Some of Apple's longtime rivals called the computer "clownish" and "silly" and the vision "far too grand."

The public? They embraced the vision and the life that it promised. And Apple Computer, now simply Apple, has seen its share price increase 4,856 percent. The closest competitor has increased approximately 14 percent.

Why?

Is it because other computer companies would prefer no one buy their products? Of course not—they all want to be successful. They all want to be well liked. What they are after is more and more influence in the form of people consuming their products.

The difference is that Steve Jobs recognized something Dale Carnegie championed repeatedly: to influence others to act, you must first connect to a core desire within them.

This is a universal truth whether you are dealing with children or clients or calves. One day the famous philosopher Ralph Waldo Emerson and his son were trying to get a calf into the barn. It was going rather poorly. They pushed and the calf pulled. They pulled and the calf pushed.

Meanwhile, their housemaid noticed their predicament, and though she couldn't write brilliant essays or books, she possessed an insight she thought might solve the problem. She walked over to the calf and put her finger in its mouth. While the calf suckled, she gently led it into the barn.

What did the maid know that the luminous philosopher had forgotten?

She knew that one of the calf's core desires was food. Once she tapped into that desire, the calf willingly followed.

Emerson and his son merely thought about what they desired—the calf in the barn so they could eat their lunch. But the calf, happily grazing in a green pasture, had little interest in descending into a dark, confined barn that curtailed his dining options. That is, until the housemaid showed up, offered her finger, and reminded the calf that some warm milk was in his future.

It is an excellent metaphor because it reminds us of two key insights we often overlook when trying to influence others.

1. Influence requires more intuition than intellect. The critical contrast between the luminary Emerson and his humble housemaid is not one of dissimilar brainpower. While Emerson was likely the more learned of the two, the divergence between them was one of intuition. The housemaid had what Emerson lacked.

The public world tends to freely ascribe sway to those in lofty positions that require much education and aptitude—the CEO, department chair, physician, and billionaire. We assume such people can move majorities with a whisper and the snap of a finger. But as Guy Kawasaki, former chief evangelist at Apple, pointed out, "If such a person does not have a deep relationship with people, she won't have much influence with them."[2]

The truth is that such stately individuals possess merely above-average conditions to influence, while the way in which influence is won remains no different for them than for anyone else. Influence is no respecter of education or experience; it goes only with the one who will set aside his status—be it high and mighty or low and lowly—and put himself in the place of another. To do so takes a shrewd and spontaneous ability to read beneath the surface of an interaction. "What is essential," wrote Antoine de Saint-Exupéry, "is invisible to the eye." This is an important truth to keep in mind when dealing with those you would like to win over. Influencing others is not a matter of outsmarting them. It is a matter of discerning what they truly want and offering it to them in a mutually beneficial package.

"He knows so little and accomplishes so much," Robert McFarlane, the third of President Reagan's six national security advisors, once marveled of his boss. When Reagan "left Washington more popular than when he first took office," writes Richard Norton Smith, he accomplished something that hadn't been done since Dwight Eisenhower.[3] How? According to President Obama, "Reagan recognized the American people's hunger for accountability and change. . . . He tapped into what people were already feeling."[4]

2. Influence requires a gentle hand. There were Emerson and his son in a four-handed, eight-legged tug-of-war with the obstinate calf who was holding his ground. It is no way to sway another to your side. Onto the scene, in great contrast, strides the housemaid with an index finger extended, straight and not hooked no less, and the once stubborn calf is suddenly light on its hooves and willingly wrapped around the housemaid's pointer.

Lest we forget, it is a memorable image of what little moving we have to do to move another to action. As a constant reminder, former U.S. president Dwight Eisenhower displayed a paperweight in the Oval Office that, in Latin, read: "Gently in manner, strong in deed."[5] There is no question of his global influence.

"Action springs from what we fundamentally desire," author Harry Overstreet writes in *Influencing Human Behavior*. "And the best piece of advice which can be given to would-be persuaders, whether in business, in the home, in the school, in politics, is: First, arouse in the other person an eager want. He who can do this has the whole world with him. He who cannot walks a lonely way."[6]

The practice of connecting with core desires is applicable across industry lines and international borders. It is as important for the energy executive from Holland as it is the executive producer in Hollywood. The interpersonal efforts that inevitably succeed are those in which the messenger stops dictating and starts discovering what the recipient wants. The interpersonal efforts that inevitably fail, be they corporate collaboration, personal cooperation, or artistic rendering, are those in which the messenger attempts to tell the recipient what he wants. This is perhaps no more evident than in the sales industry, an industry of which, in a semantic sense, we are all part.

In his book *Killing the Sale* bestselling author Todd Duncan describes the ten fatal mistakes salespeople make. One of them he calls "arguing," and when we fail to connect with another's core needs we are just as guilty of it, whether or not we call selling our profession.

> The mistake of arguing . . . is staking your sales success on your ability to state your case in convincing fashion. It's mastering a monologue and then expecting the jury of your prospects to be convinced to take your side. But . . . establishing an initial level of trust takes more than flowery monologue. It takes dialogue. It takes actual conversation. There is no other way for you to know your product or service will meet [a person's] needs.[7]

He later cites Dr. Theodore Zeldin, author of *Conversation*, who makes the point succinctly: "Real conversation catches fire."[8]

It is mind-boggling that despite the millions of branding and marketing dollars spent every year, much is still spent on the messengers' wants or whimsies rather than the recipients' core desires. We get an idea in our head for who we want to be or how we want others to perceive our offering, and we spend more time shaping and shining that image than we do ascertaining whether the image really matters to those to whom it must matter. Most individuals and organizations invest more resources in campaigning than in connecting. It should be the other way around.

Consider the comparison chart Duncan offers juxtaposing what the two forms of interpersonal communication say about you:[9]

Dialogue	Monologue
Considerate	Conceited
Authentic	Fake
Transparent	Manipulative
Secure	Needy
Interested in meeting needs	Interested in making money
Builds trust	Builds tension

Of course, connecting to people's core desires does not mean the world will be your oyster. Suffice it to say that without this approach, others will remain largely unapproachable. Their ears will close and their eyes will look elsewhere for something or someone more engaging. And their options are endless in the very world Steve Jobs saw in 2002.

Fortunately, most corporate emails, company tweets, brand blog entries, and commercial ad campaigns are monologues meant to broadcast opinions, distinguish brands, launch products, and construct personas. It is precisely because this is so that the person who speaks in a spirit of dialogue and altruistic discovery nabs a significant advantage.

How do you know if you hold this advantage?

An honest inventory of your impact is usually enough. Have your employees really stepped it up, or do they remain in a cycle of fits and falters? You are confident your marriage is on the upswing, but what does your spouse have to say? You insist the customers are impressed by your new products; does your sales revenue concur? You say your brand is sweeping the nation, but against what standard are you measuring brand recognition?

In *The Seven Arts of Change,* author David Shaner clarifies the difference between those who truly connect with core desires and those who are merely playing influence the way kids play doctor. He writes,

> Nearly every study of organizational change over the past two decades indicates that companies fail to make the change they intend approximately seventy percent of the time. . . . Before organizational change can succeed, it must first occur at the subtle spiritual level in the individuals of the organization. . . . All lasting transformation must begin there because, ultimately, your spirit and mine is the primary driver of all our behavior.[10]

True change is born of an interpersonal reach that takes hold of the deepest part of an individual. Shaner's explanation is dead on, and he should know. His company, CONNECT Consulting, has for thirty years helped multinational corporations such as Duracell, Ryobi, MARC USA, and SVP Worldwide lead successful company change efforts. His words remind us that no companywide campaign or individual communication strategy garners influence until it connects with people at their core. It is an essential principle in all your efforts to influence others, whether your audience is a five-year-old child or five thousand employees.

A former U.S. secretary of education once recounted how he didn't learn this essential element of engagement until after his first year on the job.

He felt pretty good about his progress. He'd ventured out and given speeches, and people had applauded and smiled. He'd attended many dinner parties and sumptuous gatherings, and all seemed to go off without a hitch. But to what end?

While home over Christmas with time to reflect, he came to acknowledge that while he'd been highly visible and highly promissory, nothing in the department had really changed. Five thousand employees showed up on time. They completed their assigned work. They went home. There was movement, but few if any were moved, inside or outside the office walls.

He wanted to understand why. Over the first two months of the following year he spent a lot of time with the people who really ran the Department of Education—the career civil service workers who pressed forward no matter which political party filled the White House. He came to the sobering realization that while he stood on the bridge, turning the wheel, the wheel wasn't connected to anything below. And since he had no authority to hire or fire from the civil service ranks, the only way he could influence positive progress in the department was by winning them over. The problem was, they'd seen politicians come and go. They'd grown tired and cynical. They'd given up on deriving inspiration from the top.

The secretary's wife suggested the way to win them over was by reminding them he was passionate about education, and to do so not with new words but with new actions. "Go to schools, spend time with kids. Do retail. Everyone will notice because these are the things they really care about."

"I don't do retail," he huffed. "I'm the secretary of education. I do wholesale."

His wife, the daughter of a salesman, smiled. "Darling," she said, "if you can't do retail, you'll never do wholesale."

She was right, and the secretary knew it.

For the next year he toured the country, rolled up his sleeves, read stories, listened to teachers, and was reminded how much he loved retail education. It was a personal victory. More significant, however, was the effect his actions had on his employees. Their passion was revived—passion for their daily tasks, for better education, for more opportunities for more families. They were inspired by the secretary's work because his actions had accomplished something the speeches and sumptuous gatherings had not. They had tapped a core desire of the tireless Department of Education workers: purpose. They wanted to believe again. They just needed to be reminded that their work still mattered. The secretary offered this reminder, and it dramatically turned the tide.[11]

In our rushed world, it is easy to forgo the secretary's level of analysis. So much of our digital communication is one-way that we come to believe we have limited opportunity to uncover another's perspective. While we communicate with more and more people every day, we also become more insular in our approach. We are far more inclined to focus on how we can best broadcast our points from our own perspective, quickly, broadly, or both. Isn't this what we witness all around us?

It is easy to get so caught up in the fray that we forget what we are aiming for: connection, influence, agreement, collaboration. We can start to believe the battle is won by mere frequency and occasional originality—useful strategies in the right context, but greatly insufficient as your only influence strategies.

There is a good side, however, to this constant barrage of one-sided broadcasting, which spans the spectrum from corporate posturing to celebrity positioning. Today, with a few keystrokes, we can better educate ourselves about other people's perspectives and goals.

Earlier we discussed the dangers of using your digital space to spout off your complaints. Most of us are more discerning about what we divulge. We reveal what matters to us, what we think about often, what we love and like and hope to see happen soon. These tidbytes of information add up to a body of knowledge that offers clues or even clear windows to our core desires. This knowledge is invaluable where influence in concerned because, like the calf that just wanted more food, we only move toward what moves us.

Part 2

Six Ways to Make a Lasting Impression

1

Take Interest in Others' Interests

When it comes to learning the quickest way to win friends, shall we turn to the person with the most followers on Twitter, the blogger with the most Diggs, the savviest salesperson, or the most powerful politician?

While each can boast of abundant followership, and while each will likely offer good advice, such people might not be our best role models. In fact, our best role models might not be people at all. Perhaps dogs are.

Whether we've stepped outside for two minutes or traveled for two weeks, dogs welcome our return as if we were heroes. They never demean us or mock us or stand us up for dates. They exist to befriend us, to orbit around us as the center of their existence. Are they ever without pure joy just being in our presence?

Dogs are called man's best friend for a reason. Stories of canine loyalty are the stuff of legend. The great poet Byron wrote of his dog Boatswain, "He had all the virtues of man and none of his vices."[1] These are also the stories of our day. Jon Katz's *A Dog Year* and John Grogan's *Marley & Me* were nothing if not love stories written by men grieved by their dogs' passing.

Dogs know by some divine instinct that you can make more friends in minutes by becoming genuinely interested in other people than you can in months of trying to get other people interested in you. It is more than a furry, four-legged platitude. It is a primary principle without which no person can gain real relational traction with another. The great irony of human relations—especially when viewed through the lens of a canine—is that our longing for significance in the lives of others should be so simple to meet, yet we complicate the matter; our biggest struggle is selfishness, the single greatest deterrent to amity.

That we are interested primarily in ourselves is not a phenomenon as new as Twitter or Facebook. It predates Friendster and MySpace. It came before cell phones and email and the Internet. In the 1930s, when Carnegie was penning the original manuscript of this book, the New York Telephone Company made a detailed study of telephone conversations to find out which word was the most frequently used. The personal pronoun "I" was used 3,900 times in 500 telephone conversations.

Our selfishness, or more politely our self-interest, populates the morals of the great fables. Icarus swoops and soars into the sun's warmth, melting the wax on his wings, sending him plummeting to the ocean below because he's thinking only of himself, ignoring the pleas of his father. Peter Rabbit incurs Mr. McGregor's wrath by ignoring his mother's commands to stay out of his garden. Why did Adam and Eve disobey God in the Garden of Eden? They were thinking only of themselves.

This self-interest isn't something anyone is likely to change. It is a gravitylike reality. We are born with innate fight-or-flight tendencies. That is to say, our body of words and actions trends toward self-preservation. Yet we often forget to consider whom we are really fighting against and to what destination we are fleeing.

If we are not mindful, our self-defense can turn into self-detention, keeping us from meaningful interaction and in some cases cutting us off from interpersonal progress altogether.

If we are not mindful, the destination to which we flee can become a lonely, isolated isle.

Like the city of Troy whose walls of great defense became the source of its great demise, we can insulate ourselves to the point of interpersonal futility.

"It is the individual who is not interested in his fellow men," wrote Alfred Adler, the famous Austrian psychotherapist, "who has the greatest difficulties in life and provides the greatest injury to others. It is from such individuals that all human failures spring."

That's quite an audacious statement. But it is a statement borne out in fact. Humanity's greatest failures, from the killing fields of Cambodia to the collapse of Lehman Brothers, are the result of people interested only in themselves, damn the collateral damage.

These are extreme examples, but the everyday versions are just as disturbing. The general counsel busted for taking a bribe never thought of the shareholders who were counting on that stock for their retirement. The pro athlete who took performance-enhancing drugs never considered how his actions would affect his teammates, his team's future, or the sport he claims to love. The husband and father caught in his lie was more interested in preserving a double life than protecting his family's hearts.

Still, self-preservation's downfall is about more than catastrophes. Look back at the quote "It is the individual who is not interested in his fellow men who has the greatest difficulties in life." Adler is simply explaining that a self-centered life is the most problematic life one can live. A life lived in constant interpersonal struggle. Few true friends. Shallow, short-lived influence.

This can seem a foreboding principle to embody in an age in which we are rewarded for brooding over and broadcasting our interests far and wide. But the ancient maxim is still true: "For whoever exalts himself will be humbled, and whoever humbles himself will be exalted."[2] Our effectiveness with others is ultimately a matter of motive and merchandise. Why, in the end, are you communicating and what, in the end, are you promoting? Today people are more informed and subsequently more intuitive than ever. Most of us immediately see through a person whose messaging is only for personal benefit. We see gimmicks a mile away. We run from underhanded approaches. Instead, we gravitate to what feels real and lasting. We embrace those whose messaging offers mutual benefit.[3]

Andrew Sullivan, one of the world's top political bloggers, has considered such matters for more than a decade. Once the youngest-ever editor in chief of the venerable *New Republic,* Sullivan was diagnosed HIV-positive in the early 1990s, when it was still a death sentence. After leaving that post, Sullivan became one of the Internet's first big political bloggers, with his site hitting more than 300,000 unique visitors per month in 2003.

One of the things that set Sullivan apart from his peers was an intentional interaction with his readership. He wanted his blog, *The Daily Dish,* to be about more than politics; he wanted loyal readers, and he genuinely wanted to know more about the people who followed him.

He came up with the idea for "View from Your Window," in which he asked his readers to submit shots of the world outside their homes. As with most things on the Internet, he had no idea if it would hit. "I wanted to see their worlds," he explained, "I was giving all of these people all of this access to mine, but one-way interactions are ultimately boring."[4] It was no small gesture, and it soon boosted his relationships with readers. After the gregarious feature was introduced, Sullivan's work became the centerpiece for the *Atlantic Monthly*'s online strategy, and that site's traffic increased by 30 percent. It is no surprise that Sullivan's robust blog following remained when he moved his blog to *Newsweek* and *The Daily Beast*. People are attracted to people who care about what interests them.

The irony of this principle—take interest in others' interests—is that its effectiveness is predicated on others thinking of themselves. Its effectiveness essentially requires others being self-interested. There are two things to say about this.

First, self-interest in its purest form is part of human nature—fight or flight is fact. This principle does not deny self-interest's existence in all our lives. Instead it indicates that most people, on most days, forget the other side of the human equation—everyone else. Most take self-interest to the self-centered end of the spectrum. The effectiveness of this principle is therefore tied directly to the infrequency with which most choose to think outside themselves on most days. The one who chooses, conversely, to take interest in other's interests on a daily basis is set apart. We remember such people, befriend them, and come to trust them more deeply. Influence is ultimately an outcropping of trust—the higher the trust, the greater the influence.

Second, the pinnacle of this principle is not complete self-denial. Notice the principle does not read, "Replace your interests with others' interests." It instead reads, "Take interest in others' interests," and that is the secret to its application. When you incorporate others' interests into your own—not merely for the sake of clarifying your market or ascertaining your audience—you find that your interests are met in the process of helping others.

Consider bestselling author Anne Rice, who has sold more than 110 million books in her lifetime. Her career began and achieved sustained success with her famed vampire books, including *Interview with a Vampire,* which was made into a major motion picture. While she is a uniquely gifted writer, no small part of her success has been her genuine interest in her readers. She responds to every bit of her readers' mail. This meant, at one time, employing three people full-time to meet the demand.

Her interest in others has never been feigned for the sake of book sales. "It seemed to me," she explains, "that people were kind and generous enough to have an interest in me. How could I not respond? I wanted people to know that I appreciated their letters and I appreciated them."[5]

Rice has recently taken to Facebook and Twitter, giving her more direct contact with her fans. "Oh, it's so wonderful," she said. "We're having a conversation about oh so many things."[6]

She calls the community "People of the Page" and wrote recently, "I think we must remember that Facebook, and the Internet, are what we make of them. This page has accomplished something extraordinary and perhaps unique. It is truly a community, infinitely more powerful than the sum of its parts, and I thank you for making it what it is: for participating here in so many vital and inspiring discussions."[7]

This result is as important for the owner of a business as it is for authors and bloggers.

In his cult favorite treatise, *Bass-Ackward Business,* business owner Steve Beecham summarily admits,

> I have never considered myself a brilliant businessman. . . . The country was experiencing one of the great refinance booms of all time and . . . I jumped in with both feet. Unfortunately, the refinance well dried up before my feet got wet. I went six months without a deal and when I did finally close one it was for my brother's home. . . . Instead of starting over, I set out

to find a way to make the business work. This is when my fate started to turn.[8]

Beecham had already failed in two previous business ventures—a retail store and a recycling enterprise—prior to his attempt in the mortgage business. He had every reason to pack it up and head back to school or consider letting someone else hold the reins. He resisted long enough to see that his approach was wrong from the beginning. He was after business when he should have been after relationships.

He goes on to describe an unexpected encounter in a parking lot with a selfless celebrity that taught him the visceral value of taking interest in others' interests:

> Before I could get another word in, he started asking me questions . . . Where'd you grow up? What do you do for a living? What high school did you go to? What are your kids' names? I left the encounter feeling ten feet tall. . . . In a subtle and unassuming way, he'd elevated himself in my mind.

The encounter taught Beecham an invaluable lesson. From that day forward, he committed to asking thoughtful questions of every new person he met and every acquaintance he didn't know very well. "Specifically," he explains, "I decided to become a problem solver and a promoter . . . with no strings attached. This is when my business began to not only turn around; it began to take off."

In a matter of months Beecham's job turned into a lucrative career, and soon he became so successful he owned a mortgage company that has since its inception remained at the top of the industry. Perhaps more significant is that his business has been 100 percent referral-based for a decade. He estimates that each day one-quarter of the calls his office receives have nothing to do with obtaining a mortgage—something he's very proud of. They are people calling with questions like "Where should I get my car repaired?" "Where should I take my in-laws to dinner?" and "Whom should I call for life insurance?"

He explains that these people call him because he's become known as the go-to guy in a large local network of friends. "I didn't get that way by holding free mortgage seminars or erecting a large billboard featuring my confident, trustworthy face," quips Beecham. "I got that way by helping people without hustling them for business. It is why Thoreau wrote, 'Goodness is the only investment that never fails.'"[9]

The same spirit of relating is within reach of every one of us in every interaction. How simple it is to set out motivated only to get to know others and find a problem you can help solve or a pursuit you can help promote. This is the simple secret to what Beecham calls bass-ackward business. Yet the truth is that the typical ways most conduct themselves in business relationships is what's backward.

"I'll scratch your back if you scratch mine"—this isn't reciprocity, it's bartering, an entirely different trajectory that removes the magic. And it's unadulterated magic that makes interactions so memorable. It's what draws us in. There is trust and a genuine sense of belonging and meaning.

Today there is simply no excuse not to take an interest in others' interests. Even if you are not actively involved in clubs, groups, or local organizations where face-to-face interactions are possible, there is still an abundance of opportunities to learn about others' passions and concerns. What could happen if you spent five minutes every day reading through the Facebook page of three friends, the professional biographies of three clients, or the personal blogs of three employees you haven't taken the time to know well? For starters, you'd certainly learn something about them you didn't know before. It's also likely you would come to appreciate them more. Perhaps you have similar interests; this is fodder for future conversation, even for future collaboration. Perhaps one is going through a difficult time; this is an opportunity to engage them with encouragement and a greater level of empathy. Perhaps you have a mutual friend; wouldn't this make your relationship much easier, as trust is already established in a common friend and time is already invested in common experiences? One can never underestimate the importance of affinity.

"We tend to dislike what we don't know," blogged Amy Martin, founder of social media powerhouse Digital Royalty and one of *Forbes* magazine's "20 Best-Branded Women on Twitter," after her first experience with NASCAR.[10] "Many people don't understand, or better yet 'get' . . . the so-called monotonous day of left turns and mullets." She was admittedly in that camp before attending the 2011 Daytona 500. Shortly thereafter she wrote a blog post singing NASCAR's praises for achieving a level of genuine connection and influence with its fan base that is rare in professional sports.

"Here's what I learned," she writes. "Drivers do fan Q&As and autograph sessions the day of the race. The Daytona 500 happens to be the biggest day of the year for NASCAR. I don't think Brett Favre was chatting it up with thousands of fans the day of the Super Bowl. I received a magical 'hot pass' and could go anywhere. It was uncomfortably exciting having unlimited access and at times I worried about getting in the crew's way. I was a part of the action and wasn't the only one. Bottom line, fans have access."

As for why Martin believes NASCAR's approach is a smart move for any sport, she cites the following reasons:

- Access leads to connection. (Fans are able to sign the actual racetrack.)
- Connection leads to relationships. (At all ages.)
- Relationships lead to affinity. (You can't fake this affinity.)
- Affinity leads to influence. (There's a reason so many brands are attracted to NASCAR.)
- Influence leads to conversion. (These fans would likely buy anything this driver is selling.)

Martin ends her post with a nod to the potential reach of NASCAR's genuine connectivity with its fan base—150,000 fans in the stands and 30 million television viewers—were they to embrace the opportunities the digital age affords them. "There is huge potential," she writes, "when you apply this same access via social media to a larger audience. What if the same behind-the-scenes access available to fans physically at the Daytona 500 was available to those billions of potential fans [on Facebook, Twitter, and YouTube] who are not watching the race on TV?"[11]

Martin's post bridges the two key points of taking interest in others' interests today:

1. Human relations are always easier when they begin from a place of affinity.
2. The potential for relational connectivity is astronomical.

The bottom line is that you must become genuinely interested in others before you can ever expect anyone to be interested in you. "All things being equal," said author John Maxwell in a recent interview, "people do business with people they like. All things not being equal, they still do." We like people who like us. So to be liked, you must exhibit admiration for the things others do and say.

Many have argued that people no longer have much interest in others. The "me" focus dominates how we think, act, and communicate. Yet you have so many opportunities to stay connected, to learn more, to show your interest. Changing how you spend just a small portion of each day can dramatically change how others perceive your level of interest in them. Changing your customer engagement strategy can dramatically change how the marketplace perceives your company.

Instead of spending each day refining your digital media, spend time relating to your friends, colleagues, and clients. Post brief, admiring notes. Interact with them and discover what problems you might help solve or what pursuits you might help promote; we are all driven by pain and pleasure, so such prospects exist in every person. When you are sincere in your endeavors to connect with others, chances are always higher that meaningful connection will occur. Progressive, mutually beneficial collaboration is then possible. And today, genuine connection and collaboration can quickly become infectious.

2

—

Smile

Getting people to agree about virtually anything is practically impossible. Take Neil Armstrong's 1969 romp across the moon. In the United Kingdom only 75 percent of people believe it actually happened.[1] Only 94 percent of Americans believe it happened.[2] In countries such as Mexico, China, and Indonesia, fewer than a third of respondents believe al Qaeda had anything to do with the 9/11 attacks in New York City and Washington, D.C. In the United States 16 percent of people believe it was planted explosives rather than burning passenger jets that brought down the twin towers of the World Trade Center.[3] About half of citizens in the European Union believe in God.[4]

There is one thing that does unite us, however. According to the American Academy of Cosmetic Dentistry, 99.7 percent of adults believe a smile is an important social asset.[5] It's a difficult statistic to refute, even if you aren't in the business of perfecting smiles.

We gravitate to grins and giggles. Consider the all-time most viewed videos on YouTube. The top two are all about smiles. In the most viewed, from the United Kingdom, Harry, a three-year-old boy, and his one-year-old brother, Charlie, are playing for the camera when Charlie grabs one of Harry's fingers and shoves it in his mouth. A moment later he chomps down and Harry yelps in displeasure, retrieving his finger. All the while, Charlie smiles. That smile eventually wins as Harry's smile returns and giggles ensue.[6] The other video is from Sweden. In it a baby boy smiles, giggles, and laughs in response to his parents' silly sounds. It is nearly two minutes of face-cramp-inducing smiles.[7] A combined half a billion views tell us all we need to know. Smiles send a message we like to receive.

Smiling is innate, says Daniel McNeill, author of *The Face: A Natural History*. Some sort of smile, he writes, first appears two to twelve hours after birth. No one knows whether these smiles have any content—McNeill suspects they do not—but studies show they are crucial to bonding. What no one can debate, however, is the power of a smile no matter its origin.

McNeill notes that while "courtroom judges are equally likely to find smilers and nonsmilers guilty, they give smilers lighter penalties, a phenomenon called the 'smile-leniency effect.'"[8]

Smiles also have a proliferation effect. Nicholas Christakis, a physician and sociologist at Harvard, and James Fowler, a political scientist at the University of California, San Diego, with special expertise in social networks, published a paper in the *British Medical Journal* in 2008, entitled "Dynamic Spread of Happiness in a Large Social Network." They knew emotions could spread over short periods of time from person to person, in a process known as "emotional contagion." But what they wanted to know was just how widely and sustainably happiness spread in social networks.

They followed 4,739 people from 1983 to 2003. These individuals were embedded in a larger network of 12,067 people, each having an average of eleven connections to others (including friends, family, coworkers, and neighbors), and their happiness was assessed every few years using a standard measure.

The researchers' findings confirmed the impact of a happy person, which smiling conveys directly. Social networks, they concluded,

> have clusters of happy and unhappy people within them that reach out to three degrees of separation. A person's happiness is related to the happiness of their friends, their friends' friends, and their friends' friends' friends—that is, to people well beyond their social horizon. We found that happy people tend to be located in the center of their social networks and to be located in large clusters of other happy people. And we found that each additional happy friend increases a person's probability of being happy by about 9%. For comparison, having an extra $5,000 in income (in 1984 dollars) increased the probability of being happy by about 2%. Happiness, in short, is not merely a function of personal experience, but also is a property of groups.[9]

But what of life since 2003? Do our more prominent and ever-present digital walls filter out emotions rather than encourage them? Can happiness still spread in a world of bits and bytes? The answer, they found, is yes—if we can see that people are smiling.

Christakis and Fowler followed up their first study by looking at a group of 1,700 college students interconnected by Facebook. They reviewed their online profiles, determined their closest friends, and this time studied everyone's photographs, noting those who were smiling in the photos and those who were not. They then mapped the pictures based on who was smiling and who was not. Each student was represented by a node and each line between two nodes indicated that the connected individuals were tagged in a photo together. Students who are smiling (and surrounded by smiling people in their network) were colored yellow. Students who were frowning (and surrounded by the same countenance) were colored blue. And finally, green nodes indicated a mix of smiling and non-smiling friends.

The map showed in vivid fashion how strongly the yellow nodes (smilers) and blue nodes (frowners) clustered together, with the yellow clusters proving to be much larger and more populated than the blues. Additionally, the nonsmilers seemed to be "located more peripherally in the network," primarily on the outskirts of the map.

This came as no surprise to Christakis and Fowler, who noted,

> Statistical analysis of the network shows that people who smile tend to have more friends (smiling gets you an average of one extra friend, which is pretty good considering that people only have about six close friends). Not only that, but the statistical analyses confirm that those who smile are measurably more central to the network compared to those who do not smile. That is, if you smile, you are less likely to be on the periphery of the online world.

In their final thoughts after noting the large and frequent number of node clusters surrounding smiling people, and the remote and peripherally peppered nodes of frowning people, they wrote, "It thus seems to be the case, online as well as offline, that when you smile, the world smiles with you."[10]

There is a simple reason for this phenomenon: when we smile, we are letting people know we are happy to be with them, happy to meet them, happy to be interacting with them. They in turn feel happier to be dealing with us. To someone who has seen a dozen people frown, scowl, or turn their faces away, your smile is like the sun breaking through the clouds. Your smile is often the first messenger of your goodwill.

Of course we don't always feel like smiling, but if we make the effort, we not only make those around us happier but also become happier ourselves. You may not be a particularly exuberant, outgoing person, but a simple smile takes little effort—and the rewards can be astonishing.

For the past decade, as email and texting have supplanted oral communication, we've been seduced by the fallacious notion that we live in an emotional desert. Entrepreneurs, business owners, and many professionals can carry on business with only a minimum of tactile interaction. Many modern two-dimensional media allow all of us at one time or another to forget about the importance of a smile.

In many ways texts and emails of today are like the telegraph messages of old, which had their own share of troubles. A reporter once telegraphed actor Cary Grant about his age. "HOW OLD CARY GRANT?" the message read.

The actor replied, "OLD CARY GRANT FINE. HOW YOU?"

Clearly the human proclivity toward misunderstanding is high. Throw in technology and it becomes all the more inevitable. Where telegrams were once ubiquitous, today's technology can be suffocating.

In 1929, at the telegram's peak, 200 million of them were sent. By April 2010 nearly 300 billion email messages were sent every day.[11] Pile on a daily worldwide barrage of text messages, instant messages, and Facebook wall posts, and it is a small wonder the world hasn't descended into anarchy.

Thank goodness for smiles, which can do a better job of clarifying our messages than anything—even if they take the form of traditional emoticons, little faces composed of ordinary keyboard characters designed to give much-needed context for our communications.

Recognizing the limitations of these symbols, the three largest Japanese cell phone companies—NTT DoCoMo, au, and Soft-Bank Mobile—created emojis, color pictures displaying a broad range of emotions and symbols to better emulate the face-to-face experience. Google has now adopted them for its email platform, and they are being rapidly integrated into iPhones. Yet while these clever little symbols are endearing, they are unlikely to appear within your next digital message to a board member, a problem employee, or a prospective client. Emoticons are largely for use in casual conversations, and in such contexts they serve well. How, then, do we smile across all media and, when necessary, maintain a certain level of professionalism in the process?

There is little doubt that letting another see your smile is most effective, but because so many of our interactions today are not face-to-face, you must turn your resources toward overcoming the obstacles to exhibiting friendliness across digital space. It may be simpler than you think.

Outside of emoticons and emojis, there is only one medium in which you can convey a digital smile—your voice, whether it is written or spoken. How you write an email, the tone you use, and the words you choose are critical tools of friendliness and subsequent influence. Your written words are like the corners of your mouth: they turn up, they remain straight, or they turn down. The subsequent effect—whether the words garner friendships and influence—has much to do with the linear trajectory of the emotion they convey.

Smile through your written words and you convey to others that their well-being is important to you. You and your message will have the best chance of being received. Frown through your words and others will often frown on the message and messenger.

These conclusions certainly do not account for those occasions when a more serious tone ought to be taken. Still, a good rule of thumb here is to make sure the linear thread of the message trends upward. Always begin and end the message on a positive note rather than on a pessimistic or detached one. Between two people there is nearly always a reason to smile. If you can't see a reason, then perhaps you need to wait before you write or not write at all. As many relationships have been damaged by insensitive, knee-jerk notes as by verbal insults or tirades.

The reason is simple: Written words and their effect are permanent and largely irrefutable. While you might argue against your email's negative or tactless tone, the echoing effect it has on its recipient is nearly impossible to silence. And today that effect can multiply quickly, damaging relations between employees, departments, and even entire value chains.

According to a recent issue of *Fast Company,* "New research is adding a Twittery flavor to the old adage 'birds of a feather flock together,' because it suggests happy twitterers tend to aggregate." The article goes on to explain, "Above many other factors that cause people to aggregate together, people who are sad or happy tend to communicate on Twitter with other people who are sad, or happy."

The research team, including University of Indiana professor Johan Bollen, analyzed the tweet streams from 102,000 Twitter users over six months, examining 129 million tweets.

The analysis used standard algorithms borrowed from psychological research to assess the "subjective well-being" of users from their tweets by looking for trends in positive or negative words. Then they looked at aggregation trends, and found that happier people are more usually found re-tweeting and messaging other Twitter users who are also happy. The same is true for unhappy people.

From the findings, Bollen suggests a tweet is more infectious than we realize, "and very effectively communicates joy or sadness. People who are happy would then tend to prefer (on average) happier fellow tweeters because they echo their own emotions."[12]

The fact remains—if you can't convey the proper amount of positive emotion in a written note, you are better off leaving the page blank, or perhaps even inserting an emoji (to the detriment of your professional reputation). There are worse things, in other words, than being thought a bit unprofessional. Avoiding negative sentiment with your written words altogether is obviously the goal. It is largely possible. Perhaps it is time to rethink the value of those writing skills your teachers insisted would be necessary one day. They were right, after all.

The other way in which you convey your digital voice, your spoken words, has heavy implications as well. How you speak, the tone in your voice, and the words you choose often express more than the words themselves. You have no doubt heard the retort: "Your actions speak so loudly I can hardly hear a word you are saying." It is just as true to assert: "Your tone speaks so loudly I can hardly hear a word you are saying."

Asserting you are glad to meet someone on a phone call means little if said with minimal facial movement and no positive inflection. It simply comes across that you are bored or busy with something more important, or worse, the complete opposite message—that meeting the person is an unpleasant proposition. Avoiding such situations begins in the same way it would begin if you were standing in front of the person.

Numerous studies have shown that the physical act of

smiling, even while on a phone call, actually improves the tone in which your words are conveyed. It is no coincidence that one of the central tenets that all speaking, singing, and broadcasting coaches drill into their students is that your voice sounds more pleasant, more inviting, and more compelling when you are smiling. A smile, in other words, translates across wires whether or not the person on the receiving end can see your face.

When seeking influence that leads to positive change, there is no sidestepping the door of healthy human relations. A smile opens this door whether it's visible, written, or verbal.

Rosalind Picard is a professor at the MIT Media Lab and internationally known for her book *Affective Computing*, about giving technology emotional qualities that help people communicate more effectively. The advances she highlights are nothing short of staggering—machines with "faces" that can respond appropriately to reprimands or praise, encouragement or rebuke.[13]

Of course, these machines are merely responding to preprogrammed commands, much as a computer screen responds when a key is pushed. These machines mimic physical cues, words, and verbal tone, yet they do not feel. It is worth noting that humans can program such technology. This fact alone provides compelling evidence of how well we know pat responses to others' cues, words, and tone. We are wired in the same way we wire our technologies, only with feeling to boot.

"There are two kinds of people," blogged media maven Chris Brogan,

> those who see the computer/internet/buttons as being attached to human, feeling beings, and those who think it's just online and that it doesn't attach. That's like saying the phone is just something to talk into and there's no emotions there, either. It's

not just online. People do have feelings that they associate to these "at a distance" places.

Yes, people overreact. We agree there. But to dismiss emotions simply because of the medium would be to dismiss letters, telephones, pictures, etc. Lots of things happen at a distance and yet convey consequences.

I think there are most definitely two sets of minds at work, and that by realizing the above, it describes/defines a lot of those times when one side or the other feels misunderstood. Just remembering this one detail, and realizing which of the two people you're dealing with [and which one others perceive you to be], and things might get better.[14]

Emotions, it seems, are the boundless gifts (and burdens) that humans carry. This can either discourage or encourage. Your mouth has a lot to say about your choice.

A smile, someone once said,

costs nothing but gives much. It enriches those who receive without making poorer those who give. It takes but a moment, but the memory of it sometimes lasts forever. None is so rich or mighty that he cannot get along without it and none is so poor that he cannot be made rich by it. Yet a smile cannot be bought, begged, borrowed, or stolen, for it is something that is of no value to anyone until it is given away. Some people are too tired to give you a smile. Give them one of yours, as none needs a smile so much as he who has no more to give.[15]

Smile. It increases your face value.

3

Reign with Names

On March 10, 2010, a press release skittered through the wires at Quinn Emanuel Urquhart Oliver & Hedges, one of *American Lawyer*'s top 100 law firms. John Quinn and Eric Emanuel, who founded the company twenty-five years earlier, were naming a new partner—Kathleen M. Sullivan.

Sullivan, one of the nation's top litigators and former dean of Stanford Law School, had been credentialed at Cornell, Harvard Law, and Oxford. She'd been First Lady Michelle Obama's professor at Harvard, and praise for her legal mind, acumen, and talent was universal. Her adversaries knew how tough a legal foe she was. Her appointment was well deserved.

Law firms, like all companies, make changes to their businesses from time to time. Associates come and go, paralegals and assistants as well. Partner turnover is much rarer, but it is hardly uncommon.

Why was this particular appointment so significant?

Kathleen Sullivan was not just named a partner; she became a named partner. The new firm would henceforth be called Quinn Emanuel Urquhart & Sullivan. To be a named partner in a law firm is especially significant, all the more at a prestigious firm.

But what put Sullivan's appointment into rare air was that she immediately became the first woman ever to be a named partner at one of America's top 100 law firms.

From 1870, when Ada H. Kepley became the first woman to graduate from a law school, to 2010, no other top firm had made space on its door for a woman's name. But no more. A name was embraced and a barrier broken.

Quinn wrote, "Her inclusion in the firm's name reflects the integration of our trial and appellate practices and our strengths as a national law firm." There is power in a person's name. More than a word, it is a verbal symbol of something much deeper and more meaningful. This is not just the case for groundbreakers such as Kathleen Sullivan.

From ancient to modern literature, a person's name was not merely a moniker; it was a revelation of character, personality, and fate. Apollo, Abraham, and Atticus; Cosette, Scarlett, Cinderella, and Pollyanna. In Roman times, a name was so closely identified with who a person was that when a criminal's name was removed from the civic register, all the rights of citizenship vanished. To this day certain tribes in Africa believe an individual's given name is the primary force that determines his or her skills, decisions, and ultimately life's destiny.

Is there any reason to believe a person's name is any less important today? It is perhaps more so, but it has become primarily the case in a commercial context. This represents opportunities and problems.

In the digital age, names are like company logos, identifying not only who one is but also what one represents—likes and dislikes, yeas and nays. The hundreds of millions of bloggers, tweeters, and Facebookers surely want their voices heard, but they also want their names known. Twitter and Facebook in particular have done more than simply add to an information-based economy; they have also created a new kind of name-based economy in which we are largely known by the name we brand and campaign to the world. This sort of recognition can now be monetized, of course, giving new meaning to the phrase "household name."

On Twitter and blogs, your commercial worth is commensurate with the number of names following you. As your following grows, publishing contracts, advertising agreements, and endorsement deals increase not only in viability but also in value. Technorati Top 100 blogger Ree Drummond is a great example.

A University of California, Los Angeles, graduate with big plans to practice law in a big city, she met and married her "Marlboro Man" husband while on a "pit stop" in Oklahoma, as she put it. Plans for law school in Chicago went out the window, and she moved to her husband's fourth-generation cattle ranch and took on her new moniker, "Pioneer Woman."[1] Drummond began blogging in 2006 as a way to keep friends and family apprised of her unexpected but gratifying life. By 2009 she had approximately two million readers and site traffic in the eight-figure range monthly. By 2010 she had two lucrative book contracts and two subsequent *New York Times* bestsellers, and she was earning approximately $1 million a year from blog ad sales alone.[2]

It is clear that our own names can hold value today, but lest we be tempted to forget, knowing others' names can lead to greater success. Dave Munson, founder of the Saddleback Leather Company, knows this well. He was a volunteer English teacher in Mexico when he had his first leather bag made from a design he drew for a local leatherworker. The bag garnered so much attention on his hometown streets of Portland, Oregon, he decided to return to Mexico immediately and have more made. A month later Munson returned to Portland with eight bags in tow and sold them all from the safari rack of his old Land Cruiser in three hours. The Saddleback Leather Company was born, and with it the goal "to love people around the world by making excessively high quality, tough and functional leather designs."[3]

His secret? Munson frequently fields customer calls from his cell phone and returns online questions via phone or email; he also travels to Mexico multiple times each year to stay connected with the Mexican leatherworkers still making his bags. The visits aren't showmanship. "I hug the workers and ask them how I can pray for them," he explained in a recent interview. "When I first started taking the trips I remember how shocked these men were that I would call them by name and then sit down and talk to them about their personal lives. One got tears in his eyes. Then so did I."[4]

He doesn't share these personal stories on his blog or in his marketing literature because he believes promising to do something is different from simply producing it. Saddleback is proud, he says, to remain a family business despite selling millions of dollars' worth of leather goods each year. "I've heard horror stories of lots of small and successful businesses who, driven by greed, try to become giants and fail," Munson writes on his blog. "We aren't like that. We are and will maintain our family of leather owners with love. Pretty much everyday I lay down in bed with my hot wife and we talk about different bag owners who we've been going back and forth with. We want to know your name."[5]

It is this level of personal touch—putting people's names before product names and profits—that makes one surmise Saddleback Leather will be around as long as one of his leather bags, which carries the tagline "They'll fight over it when you're dead."

The opportunities to be known by others and to know others are ultimately two sides of the same coin. There is branding—the introduction of you to others. And then there is relationship building—the interaction between you and others. What is interesting is that you can forgo the former and still be successful. You can be so good at building relationships that your interactions with others birth and sustain your brand. Conversely, you cannot sustain success on branding alone. You cannot brand yourself or your business and then forgo building relationships. In the end, business is still about one person relating to another. Mr. Bates from Watkinsville, Georgia, experienced this firsthand.

He is a business owner who always takes his top out-of-town suppliers to Bone's, a famous Atlanta restaurant some seventy miles away. His loyalty, however, wasn't born of their exquisite menu, branded as well as any in North America. It started with a waiter named James.

As Mr. Bates and a supplier pulled up to their table one evening, James approached promptly. "Hello, Mr. Bates," he said. "Thank you for choosing Bone's. It is a pleasure to have you back."

To hear Mr. Bates describe it, it was no insignificant moment. "It changed the dining experience and imprinted that restaurant in my mind. I'd only dined there once before—six months earlier— and James not only knew my name, he took the time to discover I'd been there before. I was by no means a regular, but the small gesture made me feel like one. It was the old adage about 'treating someone like the person you want him to become' coming true."

For such a small gesture it paid big dividends. "I don't take my suppliers anywhere else now," said Mr. Bates. Judging by the popularity of Bone's, it would seem many customers share his sentiment.

This is the primary business payoff of remembering people's names: they remember you. The flipside is an unenviable place to be.

One of the first lessons a politician learns is this: "To recall a voter's name is statesmanship. To forget is oblivion." It is one trait that unites most of history's great leaders. From Lincoln to Churchill to Bonaparte, these men figured out ways to remember people's names with surprising consistency. In so doing, they recalled, knowingly or not, a famous Emerson saying: "Good manners are made up of petty sacrifices."[6]

When it comes to remembering names, some sacrifices may be required. Napoleon III, emperor of France and nephew of the great Napoleon Bonaparte, claimed he could remember the name of every person he met despite all of his royal duties.

How? If he didn't hear the name distinctly, he said, "So sorry. I didn't get the name clearly." Then, if it was an unusual name, he would say, "How is it spelled?"

During the conversation, he took the trouble to repeat the name several times and tried to associate it in his mind with the person's features, expression, and general appearance. If the person was of special importance to him, he later wrote the name down on a piece of paper, looked at it, concentrated on it, fixed it securely in his mind, and then tore up the paper. In this way, he gained a visual impression of the name as well as an audible impression.[7]

Our challenges today are far greater than Napoleon's. Numerous studies show that the only thing worse than television for our attention span is the Internet. A blur of 140-word tweets, Facebook news feeds, emails, instant messages, and web pages are beginning to rewire our brains.

In a May 2010 issue of *Wired*, author Nicholas Carr revealed that a professor at the University of California, Los Angeles, had discovered that just five hours on the Internet rerouted people's neural pathways. Carr noted:

Dozens of studies by psychologists, neurobiologists, and educators point to the same conclusion: When we go online, we enter an environment that promotes cursory reading, hurried and distracted thinking, and superficial learning. Even as the Internet grants us easy access to vast amounts of information, it is turning us into shallower thinkers, literally changing the structure of our brain.[8]

In 2010 famed film critic Roger Ebert blogged, "There's such a skitterish impatience in our society right now."[9] He's right. But such reality doesn't give us an excuse for forgetting people's names. Instead, it provides us with a challenge. As more and more people find it more and more difficult to remember names, there is enormous advantage to be gained by those who do.

How?

There are some easy ways. Instead of defaulting to hollow, truncated greetings such as "Hey" or "Hi," default to a greeting that uses the person's name: "Dear Robin" or "Good morning, Robert." When you do, practice Napoleon's technique and visualize the person's face. If you've taken the advice of earlier chapters and sought to take interest in the person's interests, impress your mind with those as well. "Robert is married with three daughters and he likes reading Ernest Hemingway." It's a simple exercise that will not only help you greet Robert by name the next time you interact; it will also go a long way to helping you consistently view him outside a mere transactional context.

A quick tip here: Before you use people's names, make sure you know them in the right context. Today most people have more than one name to which they answer. Celebrated entrepreneur Richard Branson is "Richard" to many friends, but he is also "Mr. Branson" to many acquaintances and "Sir Richard" to many fellow Brits. While we are a far less formal society at large, using a person's name out of context is a good way to get a relationship off on the wrong foot. Susan or Suzie? Ben or Benjamin? Jacqueline or Jackie? The best advice is to avoid guessing.

Don't call Richard "Richie," "Rich" or "Dick" in an email unless he's been introduced as such, he's asked you to use that name, or he's referred to himself with that name in a voice mail, text message, or email to you. If you've not been introduced and have never corresponded, do a little homework on what people in your same relational position are calling him. Don't check to see what his Facebook or Twitter friends call him—at this point you're not yet his friend and have not earned the right to call him a more casual name. Instead, review how he refers to himself on his website or blog. If there is an article written about him or in which he is referenced, use that name.

We must remember that a person is more interested in his or her own name than in all the other names on earth put together. Remember that name and use it easily, and you have paid a subtle and very effective compliment. But forget it or misspell it, and you have placed yourself at a sharp disadvantage.

While many choose the safer alternative and address a person with terms such as "man," "ma'am," and "sir," you can place yourself in the same person's better graces by taking the time to not only remember but also use his or her name. Many of the salutation pitfalls we fear are easily avoidable with a few minutes' worth of research. Aren't a few minutes of your time worth it if it means standing out from the crowd, if it means making a better impression than most people make on others?

If you want others to remember and use your name, the small investment is necessary. People have names coming at them in all forms all day long—people's names, company names, brand names, street names, and store names. What will set yours apart? Largely, the emotions people associate with your name. If you're just another waiter in just another restaurant in Atlanta—a metropolitan area of more than five million people—you will be no more memorable than the numbers on your license plate or the color of your shirt. Your name will do little to trigger emotions that connect others to you. It is no coincidence that Mr. Bates easily remembered James's name after only one encounter. He estimates he dines out about twelve times a month. When asked if he remembers other waiters' names, he replied, "I barely remember my own some days."

We should always be aware of the magic contained in a person's name and realize that this word is wholly and completely owned by the person with whom we are dealing, and nobody else. It is a person's trademark. After the gift of life, a person's name is the first gift he or she received. When this word is used in conversation, the information we are discussing or the connection we are seeking takes on greater meaning.

Perhaps a doctor's office provides the best evidence. There is an ongoing debate in the medical world about how and when first names should be used. Does a first-name basis overpersonalize interactions that are best kept in a professional realm? Or would a first-name basis help in the process of health and healing and particularly in the process of discussing very difficult prognoses?

It would seem that most doctors believe professionalism is important and first names are best kept at bay. Yet doctors' offices are typically places where patients feel dehumanized. They are folders and cases, not faces and feelings. Their names are frequently mispronounced or mistaken altogether, only serving to highlight a potentially dangerous disconnection.

One high-profile doctor decided to buck the trend.[10] Dr. Howard Fine is the head of the neuro-oncology program at the National Institutes of Health. In that capacity he performs original research, oversees and distributes all of NIH's funding, and is the hands-on doctor for as many brain cancer patients as want to see him—free of charge, since it is a government program.

When patients arrive to see him for the first time, they are largely hopeless. They've seen the statistics on the Internet. They've heard horror stories. Dr. Fine views part of his job as restoring hope—responsible hope. How he handles names plays a leading role in this process.

He estimates he's seen more than twenty thousand patients over the years, and one of the ways he has chosen to interact is by introducing himself as "Howard Fine," without the doctor designation. From there his patients are encouraged to call him by his first name. It takes the relationship to another level, whereby he is no longer a detached doctor trying to keep them from dying; he is a highly educated friend, wise confidant, and fierce advocate who will fight for their full recovery. He is not in the business of blowing smoke. Instead, he understands that because the sharing of facts is both important and poignant for his patients, the establishment of rapport is essential for their well-being. What brain tumor patients need more than a doctor is a trusted advisor who understands. This is achieved more naturally when the doctor puts himself on the same level of his patients, a fellow human with a strong desire to live.

It would be easy for a prominent physician to find power in the "Dr." moniker. But a big part of what makes Fine's program the crown jewel of the National Institutes of Health, according to one of the institute's heads, is that he recognizes that first names are more powerful and purposeful than detached ranks or bestowed titles. It is why Carnegie insisted names are "the sweetest and most important sound in any language."

4
—

Listen Longer

How do you get the job, land the client, increase your influence, and not lose $180 million in market capitalization? Listen.

In March 2008 the members of a little-known indie band from Canada were on their way to Nebraska to for a weeklong tour. The first leg of their United Airlines flight landed in Chicago. As the guys began to deplane, they heard a woman behind them exclaim, "They're throwing guitars out there!" They pressed their noses up against the windows to see for themselves. The woman was right; their guitars were being tossed and dropped and tossed again onto the luggage cart.

One of those guitars, a $3,500 Taylor, belonged to the band's lead singer, Dave Carroll, who immediately tried telling a flight attendant what was happening.

On his website he explains she cut him off. "Don't talk to me," she said. "Talk to the lead agent outside."

He went outside, where another employee never took the time to listen to his complaint. A third employee dismissed him saying, "But hun, that's why we make you sign the waiver." He explained that he hadn't signed a waiver and that no waiver would excuse what many people on the plane had seen. She told him to wait until Omaha to talk to someone.[1]

Not surprisingly, when he opened his guitar case he discovered it had been badly damaged. Thus began a yearlong odyssey in which Dave Carroll tried to get someone at United Airlines to listen.

During those twelve months, every United employee Carroll spoke with told him what to do, but none bothered to listen to him. At one point they told him to bring the guitar to Chicago for inspection. He had long since returned to his home in Canada, some fifteen hundred miles away.

In the meantime, Carroll had the guitar fixed for $1,200. He was a professional musician and needed the primary tool of the trade. But the sound wasn't the same.

He told United he would settle with them for the repair bill. His request fell on deaf ears.

But a traveling songwriter always has two things: something to say and a means to say it. If United wouldn't listen, perhaps his music audience would.[2]

Carroll sat down and wrote a song called "United Breaks Guitars," and on July 6, 2009, he uploaded a video of it to YouTube. He hoped for a million views in the first year. People listened far more than he anticipated: two weeks after it premiered, the video had nearly four million views. Within days, *The Times* of London revealed, "the gathering thunderclouds of bad PR caused United Airlines' stock price to suffer a mid-flight stall, and it plunged by 10%, costing shareholders $180 million. Which, incidentally, would have bought Carroll more than 51,000 replacement guitars."[3]

The power of listening is the power to change hearts and minds. More consequentially, it is the power of giving people what they most desire—to be heard and understood.

Seesmic founder Loïc Le Meur maintains that the very idea of online ad campaigns is passé. The key for any and every company is a "long-term engagement program" that facilitates listening to customers.[4]

Online ad campaigns have so much promise, though. They can deliver a demographic profile unlike any other medium. Your company wants a twenty-three-year-old female computer programmer who likes basket weaving? There's almost certainly a site where she can be found. Such profiling has long been the dream of advertisers everywhere. How could this not work?

It doesn't work, Le Meur says, because generating impressions or exposure simply isn't how the world works.[5] Rather, it works through listening and building up trust. This process is a slow one, but one that will always bear fruit.

During the darkest hours of the Civil War, Lincoln wrote to an old friend in Springfield, Illinois, asking him to come to Washington. Lincoln said he had some problems he wanted to discuss with him. The old neighbor got to Washington as quickly as he could. Lincoln talked to him for hours about the advisability of issuing a proclamation freeing the slaves. He went over all the arguments for and against such a move, and then read letters and newspaper articles, some denouncing him for not freeing the slaves and others denouncing him for fear he was going to free them. After the long conversation, Lincoln shook hands with his old friend, said goodnight, and sent him back to Illinois without ever asking for his opinion. Lincoln had done all of the talking. But the talking seemed to clarify his mind.

"He seemed to feel easier after that talk," the old friend said. Lincoln hadn't wanted advice. He had wanted a sympathetic, trusted listener to whom he could unburden himself. Ultimately it is what we all seek at one time or another. The question is whether you are discerning enough to be a burden lifter.

When President Coolidge became vice president, Channing H. Cox succeeded him as governor of Massachusetts and came to Washington to call on his predecessor. Cox was impressed by the fact that Coolidge was able to see a long list of callers every day and yet finish his work at 5:00 p.m., while Cox found that he was often detained at his desk up to nine o'clock. "How come the difference?" he asked Coolidge. "You talk back," said Coolidge.[6]

Listening's power, like that of smiling, is strong. When you listen well you not only make an instant impression, you also build a solid bridge for lasting connection. Who can resist being around a person who suspends his thoughts in order to value yours?

Few people in modern times have listened as well as Sigmund Freud. A man who once met him described his manner of listening:

> It struck me so forcibly that I shall never forget him. He had qualities, which I had never seen in any other man. Never had I seen such concentrated attention. There was none of that piercing "soul penetrating gaze" business. His eyes were mild and genial. His voice was low and kind. His gestures were few. But the attention he gave me, his appreciation of what I said, even when I said it badly, was extraordinary. You've no idea what it meant to be listened to like that.[7]

One might argue that people such as Freud, Lincoln, and others in an age gone by had it easier. Their world was smaller and certainly more controlled. There is some truth to this argument, but not anything that provides us an excuse.

Yes, our age is broader and far more untamed, but we made it so. And it is therefore we who can make such traits work in our favor. Unfortunately, it seems many haven't yet figured it out.

While our circle of influence balloons well beyond our neighbors and work colleagues to encompass, primarily through Facebook, much of our relational history, such an expansive network that numbers in the hundreds if not the thousands seems to be overwhelming to most. While the number of people to whom we might listen has expanded, the number of people to whom we actually listen is diminishing.

A recent study profiled in the *American Sociological Review* reveals that people are growing more socially isolated than they were even twenty years ago:

> Overall, the number of people Americans have in their closest circle of confidants has dropped from around three to about two. . . . Whereas nearly three-quarters of people in 1985 reported they had a friend in whom they could confide, only half in 2004 said they could count on such support. The number of people who said they counted a neighbor as a confidant dropped by more than half, from about 19 percent to about 8 percent.[8]

"We're not saying people are completely isolated," notes Lynn Smith-Lovin, a Duke University sociologist who helped conduct the study. "They may have 600 friends on Facebook . . . and e-mail 25 people a day, but they are not discussing matters that are personally important."[9]

More so than when this book was first published in 1936, there is a crying need for people who will make the time to listen, for people who will resist the "skitterish impatience" so prevalent in our age and make people more important than progress. It is of course absurd to believe progress can be made without the fidelity of other people, but we usually don't see this until other people let us know—with their eyes, with their silence, with their closed wallets.

There are few new tips that can create a personal or corporate cache of better listening. But there is one principle that, if applied daily, can reconnect you with others on a lasting level: presence. A martyred spiritual ambassador once framed the principle this way: "Wherever you are, be all there."[10]

John, an aspiring political writer, understood this principle far earlier in life than his peers. His claim is that he's never given a bad job interview. For every interview, he's received an offer. But what is perhaps most interesting is that there has rarely been anything on paper to suggest he was the best fit. "I have, more often than not," he admits, "been an average prospect on paper."

To what, then, does he attribute his uncommon interview success rate? A counterintuitive perspective on interviews. He explains:

> Every interview is a chance to learn something new about people I've never met. Think about it; the environment is conducive to it. There's already a natural give-and-take. In my interviews I've learned about everything from culinary tastes to dashed dreams to crazy hopes. People want to be listened to and they want people around who will listen. So I listen. And I've found that listening imparts a great deal of respect—more so than any planned speech ever could.[11]

So it turns out that listening also garners great respect. And John's rare interview presence has translated into rare opportunities—he has served as both a CIA agent and a White House speechwriter.

When asked for suggestions on embodying his level of presence with others, he says his personal goal is to ask fifteen questions per day. The most important five, he explains, are to your family or those in closest proximity to you. Sure, ask about their day. But go deeper. Ask what made them laugh. Or perhaps what made them cry. Ask them about a lesson they learned or a person they met whom they liked.

The next five are for the people with whom you work on a regular basis. "The old truth that there are no bad questions may or may not be true in a brainstorming session. It is certainly true when done with sincerity in a conversation with another person. If you ask with respect and interest, you cannot go wrong."

Finally, he explains, the last five questions are for your digital space—Facebook, emails, Twitter, and blogs. "Read others' posts and messages closely; comment or reply with questions, and do it for at least five different people every day. In addition to that, use your posts and updates to ask more questions of your friends and followers. You may be surprised at how many people respond."

These are lessons Bob Taylor of Taylor Guitars certainly takes to heart. When he heard that Dave Carroll's Taylor guitar had been damaged by United Airlines, he called Carroll directly and offered him two guitars of his choice.

Imagine what might have happened if someone, anyone, at United exercised an ear for how to make things right with David Carroll. If they had, chances are high they would not have had to issue the following statement when Carroll's video went viral:

> This has struck a chord with us. We are in conversations with one another to make what happened right, and while we mutually agree that this should have been fixed much sooner, Dave Carroll's excellent video provides United with a learning opportunity that we would like to use for training purposes to ensure all customers receive better service from us.[12]

It is often said that you live and learn, but perhaps an equally important lesson for us all is that if you listen and learn, you live more harmoniously.

5

—

Discuss What
Matters to Them

At a dinner party, George Bernard Shaw sat next to a young man who proved to be a bore of historic proportions. After suffering through a seemingly interminable monologue, Shaw cut in to observe that between the two of them, they knew everything there was to know in the world.

"How is that?" asked the young man.

"Well," said Shaw, "you seem to know everything except that you're a bore. And I know that!"[1]

Not quite the impression the young man was aiming for. But it proves an important point: when it comes to mattering to others, you must discuss what matters to them. Assume all else will fall on deaf, or in this case dull, ears.

This is an interesting principle to consider given the spirit in which the vast majority of people communicate today. Most messages are primarily meant to educate others about our lives or our products, to reveal compelling portions of ourselves we think others would be attracted to. While this appears to be an assertive strategy, it is actually a passive strategy in that it requires others to connect with us. Like a banner ad on a website waiting to be clicked, we offer up digital ads of our best selves, hoping others will be compelled to engage.

The trouble is, that's marketing monologue, not relational dialogue. It's assumption, not assimilation. When assumption guides our efforts to befriend or influence others, the results end up on the wrong side of memorable.

In 1810, U.S. general William Henry Harrison, then governor of the Indiana Territory, was negotiating with Tecumseh in order to try to prevent open hostilities. He ordered a chair to be brought for the Native American chief. The man who brought it said, "Your father, General Harrison, offers you a seat."

"My father!" Tecumseh exclaimed. "The sun is my father and the earth is my mother, and on her breast I will lie." Ignoring the chair, he stretched himself out on the ground.[2]

Today's biggest enemy of lasting influence is the sector of both personal and corporate musing that concerns itself with the art of creating impressions without consulting the science of need ascertainment. Not only is this method presumptuous, but it is a poor business tack. What the world needs more of—what Carnegie espoused seventy-five years ago—is bridge-building dialogue. This begins when you flip the modern spirits of marketing and social media on their heads and begin all interactions with a mind for what matters to the other person.

This starts, as we have said, with listening. Once you know what matters to others through a practice of longer listening, you can then truly engage them by putting such matters at the forefront of your interactions. If you're talking business, this process is about putting the customer back into customer relationship management—an endeavor that blogger Doc Searls once pointed out is more often about management than the customer.[3]

"Everyone is wrong about influence," writes power blogger and business strategist Valeria Maltoni, "except your customers."

Think about that before you get into trouble for not delivering meaningful results. . . . True influence flows from drawing together people with shared interests. It's a process of identifying areas of relevancy among your customers and prospects, community building and allowing others to amplify your influence as you meet their needs. . . . You'll be chasing the popular kids (even those who demur) until the cows come home if you keep thinking that influence is about you. It's not. And you don't need the following of a celebrity to build something of significance.[4]

You are ultimately building a community when you initiate interactions with what matters to others. And a community is what really matters to you, whether you're building a brick-and-mortar business, launching a new brand, or planning an important reunion. Sure, there is an initial connection, and you need to make it. But much of marketing and social media today is only about the connection point—gaining another follower, notching another fan, claiming another customer. Often forgotten is the long-term plan. Businesses call it a customer retention strategy, but it is best thought of as a lively, meaningful dialogue among a community of friends.

If the foundation of all long-term success is the establishment of trust-based relationships, then the goal of all interactions should be to convey value as soon and as often as possible. There are common hurdles to overcome.

Jason travels to Senegal's most remote regions a few times a year. He first traveled with a nonprofit that led him there. He returns today because he still learns there. Recently one of the village elders pulled him aside on a 115-degree afternoon to ask him a most urgent question: How did people in North America live?

Jason explained that most lived in individual houses somewhat akin to the huts in the village. Others lived in apartments stacked on top of and next to each other to form bigger buildings.

"And all of these homes," the elder inquired, "they have walls all around?"

Yes, replied Jason.

"But why?"

"To keep themselves safe from bad weather and sometimes from bad people and to protect the things in their home and to give privacy."

"Oh, no, no, no," the elder replied. "That is backward." In their village, he explained, they had torn down the walls to keep themselves safe. "You see, too many things hide behind walls. If we tear down the walls for all to see, then we are all safer."

We live in a modern world, and in the modern world we put up walls. There are firewalls for our computers, mortar walls for our estates, and wood and wire fences for our farms and family yards. Then there is the great wall of diffuse social interaction. It can lead to a level of influence that exists outside relationship— an influence founded on followership but not friendship.

Open Leadership author and social media maven Charlene Li warns about the danger of such fortified digital influence. In a recent interview she noted the biggest concern—a false sense of security. "There is a difference between a friend and a fan," she explained. "Fans have a smaller sense of commitment, smaller levels of interest. There is a continuum of loyalty whereby fans stand at one end and friends at the other. Influence occurs across the continuum but it is more certain and lasting on the friends' end."[5]

The easiest way to prove Li's point is to go online and try to buy a Facebook friend. It can't be done. Companies galore will sell you Facebook fans, and they can assure you of lots of Twitter followers, but leave it to social media to shine a bright light on the great truth that no true friend can be bought.

"When are we going to learn that millions of followers does not always equal influence?" blogged Canadian Mitch Joel, author of *Six Pixels of Separation* and one of the iMedia 25: Internet Marketing Leaders and Innovators.

> It's a game (err . . . business) that worked well until the proper analytics and platforms were put in place. . . . [S]maller, stronger groups are where influence lies. . . . The brands that are winning "true influence" . . . are winning (as opposed to #winning) because they have people who are having real interactions with other real human beings (and those interactions are truly meaningful). . . . [I]t is much more practical/realistic for businesses to think about using these opportunities to connect and have a sincere engagement instead of trying to rack up their numbers.[6]

Newton Minow was the influential head of the Federal Communications Commission under President John F. Kennedy. He later went on to serve in various other prestigious public and private sector jobs. When asked what his secret was, he said that it all came down to his college major. He'd majored in semantics—the study of meaning. Semantics isn't simply about words; it's about the context in which those words are used. It's about understanding.

He once remarked that 99 percent of all conflicts are about the misunderstanding of words used in different contexts. His success, therefore, came from trying diligently to understand what someone meant.[7]

The endeavor is all the more significant today because when Mark Zuckerberg decided to call everyone on Facebook "friends" he made a semantic choice that is easily misunderstood. The human brain—to say nothing of the human heart—cannot process hundreds of friends. According to Oxford University professor of evolutionary anthropology Robin Dunbar, the size of our brain limits our ability to manage social circles to around 150 friends, regardless of our sociability.

Dunbar has looked at Facebook and found it to be true online as well. "The interesting thing is that you can have 1,500 friends but when you actually look at traffic on sites, you see people maintain the same inner circle of around 150 people that we observe in the real world."[8]

But here it is important to introduce Dunbar to Minow, because Dunbar defines a friend as someone you care about and contact at least once a year. Distinctions must be made, for while we cannot have 150 intimate friends, we can have 150 influential relationships.

Intimate friendships possess deep commitment and are based on great risk—first comes the risk of believing that we are people who matter enough, who are weighty enough, to influence others' lives. If we do not understand the significance of our presence, we can never give anyone the present of our lives. But an equally great risk is that having intimate friends opens us up to being deeply hurt by those friends. Some people protect themselves from relational pain by having no intimate friends. Others do it by having so many shallow friends that a hurt inflicted by one is diffused by the mass.

The bottom line is that relationship involves risk, and if we want to influence other people's lives, we have to be comfortable accepting that risk. While the amount we give of ourselves varies based on the relational intimacy we are seeking, risk is always implicit in the process of moving people from curious followers to certain friends with whom you have influence that transcends transactional trends. Once you know what matters to others through a practice of listening, placing your matters in a holding pattern is the only way to truly engage others with a steady diet of what they care about. And as with most meaningful risks, the reward is commensurate. Subsequent influence is more potent, and there soon comes a time when what matters to you matters to them.

Jamie Tworkowski understands. In 2002 a friend named Renee was using the same razor blade to line her cocaine and cut her arms. Depressed, alone, and surrounded by "friends" who were spiraling down with her, Renee was not long for this world.

Jamie, an unassuming surfboard sales rep, stepped in and with a group of friends intervened in Renee's world. Eschewing emotional risk, they tried to give her the gift of presence. They bought her coffee and cigarettes, they gave her music, they surrounded her with love. They wondered what it would be like if, instead of her cutting a self-loathing, four-letter moniker into her arm, they could write love on her arms.

Jamie's friendship with Renee led him to design some T-shirts to sell to support the cost of her recovery program. His friendship with the lead singer of a popular rock band led him to ask a favor of the front man: "Wear one of our T-shirts onstage." The musician did.

Nearly a decade later, Renee is clean and Jamie's organization, To Write Love on Her Arms, sells nearly $3 million in T-shirts a year and invests that money in numerous recovery programs.

More than 200,000 follow Jamie on Twitter and Facebook. But he knows most are curious fans and followers. A much smaller number are friends, such as Renee.

He has some slight influence with those who follow him; yet it is shallower than the influence he has with his friends, and mostly fleeting. He accepts this and celebrates that there are others in the world also doing good things worthy of following.

He has strong influence with his friends; this is the malleable setting in which he chooses to reside. It is this place—

different for everyone—where you must reside, whether you're a multinational corporation or an individual change agent.

The distinction between your friends and your followers is an important one to consider when seeking to make a lasting impression on others. There are those in this world with whom you have earned significant influence; they are a gift and a responsibility. You should not only know who they are but also always know what matters to them. The gift is what they bring to you; value it. The responsibility is to lead your relationship somewhere meaningful to both of you—but at the very least, to them.

"A brand's ability to have its message put in front of millions of people begins and ends with that impression," concludes Mitch Joel in his aforementioned blog post.

> We (as a public) seem to believe that the influence comes from the sheer volume of impressions and connections that we have in the marketplace. . . . It doesn't. True influence comes from connecting to the individuals, nurturing those relationships, adding real value to the other [people]'s lives and doing anything and everything to serve them, so that when the time comes for you to make an ask, there is someone there to lend a hand. Worry less about how many people you are connected to and worry a whole lot more about who you are connected to, who they are and what you are doing to value and honor them.[9]

Perhaps what is most meaningful to you, after all, is being meaningful to others. One thing is certain: In an age when the mass of messages multiplies daily, only a small number really matter. To influence others, make sure yours are among them.

6

Leave Others a Little Better

"He called himself Mike," began blogger and consummate Building Champions business coach Steve Scanlon as he relayed a story he loves to share. "My wife, Raffa, and I were staying a few blocks south of Central Park, and we'd hailed his cab to embark on an annual dining tradition in Little Italy. Our timing was terrible. It was Halloween, and the already crowded streets were twice full. As Mike chopped his way through midtown and lower Manhattan it was apparent our plans would need to change. He suggested Greenwich Village, and we agreed. A few minutes later he dropped us at a Village curb, recommended three restaurants, and then rolled back into the crawling mass. I thought it was the last we'd seen of him."[1]

But, as Scanlon likes to say with a smile, Mike thought differently.

As they enjoyed their meal, Scanlon reached for the front pocket of his pants. He patted here and there, and there and here. His phone was missing. He panicked as he suddenly remembered where it was.

Resignation set in as he imagined the misery of canceling his account, losing valuable contact information, and buying a new phone. He dialed his number from his wife's phone, expecting to hear his own recording. Instead, a gentle Indian accent answered.

"Hulloo?"

"Who's this?" Scanlon snapped, brusquer than intended.

"Thees is Mike," the voice said.

Scanlon took a breath and fumbled through an explanation that ended with them needing to catch a flight home very soon.

"My goodness," Mike replied, "your phone is very important. I will come as quickly as I can." He then coordinated a street corner meeting and promised to hurry.

Scanlon turned to his wife in amazement and relief and explained what was happening. When Mike pulled to the curb twenty minutes later and delivered the phone, Scanlon put $80 in the cabbie's hand—all the cash on him.

"He was humbled," explained Scanlon, "but I wanted him to know how outstanding the act was. He hadn't mentioned money once. Turning off his meter and going way out of his way to help an irresponsible customer was extraordinary—I'd have given him twice the cash if I had it on me."

This cabbie's small act of service made a big impact; it turned a nightmare into noteworthy experience. Scanlon calls what Mike did "small-picture thinking." It is the foundation of leaving others a little better.

Somewhere along the way, we were taught to keep the big picture at the forefront of our minds. We learned the benefits of setting big goals, making big connections and closing big deals. Today, the most common big picture may be gaining a big following. And while such big pictures have value, if our minds are focused only on big payoffs, we will overlook the small opportunities that make the biggest difference. We will miss chances to go a little deeper, to connect a little tighter, to make others feel that much better about their relationship with us.

"The point," explained Scanlon, "is not that big-picture

thinking is bad. It is a necessary piece of progress—especially with people—but it alone is not enough to reach your big goals."

Many steps come between what we sow and what we reap. Most are small seeds planted in the small moments of every day.

Consider the sales manager at Macy's who cast a big vision to double women's shoe sales in June. There would be a big summer sale, he explained, and in combination with a big push in upselling, that would turn out big results. What resulted, unfortunately, was no big deal.

June 1 came, and his sales force stopped listening to the customers' stories. They stopped being sensitive to customers' budgets and considerate of their time. Instead they began fishing for big opportunities to suggest a more expensive shoe or a half-priced second pair or a matching accessory. By month's end, total sales had decreased by 8 percent.

What went wrong?

A typical sales manager might blame his sales team for lack of execution. This particular manager pointed the finger at himself. What could he have done differently? He realized his big-picture obsession had taken his team's focus off the small actions that would make it a reality. It is a common mistake. Fortunately, this particular manager had a second chance.

A few months later, Macy's was having a Labor Day sale. The sales manager took a different approach. He painted the same big picture—double the previous month's sales—but this time he described the small details within the big picture. He asked his people to look for every opportunity to serve their customers: walk them to the bathroom, hold their babies, park their strollers behind the counter, be mindful of their time commitments and budget constraints. Instead of focusing on what they were selling, the sales team should focus on making their customers' days a little better, whether or not they bought shoes.

What do you think happened?

Total sales for September were 40 percent higher than August. It was not a doubling of sales—a goal even the manager admitted was quite lofty—but it was 50 percent better than the same effort in June. Most important, it was progress. The difference was in the details.

The big picture didn't change. The salespeople's focus did. Instead of looking for the big sell, they sought small, meaningful ways to leave people a little better. The smaller seeds sown meaningfully reaped a bigger harvest.

Many people make the mistake of equating inspiration with implementation. They are like an art teacher who sets his students down in an alpine meadow and asks them to reproduce the glorious landscape. The big picture is inspiring: long swaying grass, white aspens with shimmering golden leaves, a brook winding toward the backdrop of snowcapped mountains. But merely seeing the picture does not equip the students to skillfully depict one blade of grass on the canvas. Without instruction in painting each small detail in that big picture, their efforts will look nothing like that picturesque meadow before them. To become great artists who can replicate the big picture, the students must learn to focus on the small particulars. Nowhere in life is this truer than in human relations.

Who doesn't have grand plans for certain partnerships, collaborative efforts, or friendships? A marriage proposal is nothing if not a vision for the future of the relationship. A collaboration agreement is nothing if not a vision for the future of the business partnership. An employment agreement is nothing more than a vision of the great work an employer and employee can accomplish together. But is it enough to wax poetic about your love for the woman? Is it enough to promise great customer service, relevant content, or valuable support?

It is said that Leonardo da Vinci began painting *Mona Lisa* in

1503 and did not finish until 1519. Some art historians speculate he spent much of that span considering and crafting the enigmatic smile that has been the centerpiece of conversation for five centuries. The famous smile now adorns its own $7.5 million room in the Louvre, where 6 million visitors pay their respects each year. The painting's value is estimated in the ballpark of half a billion U.S. dollars, though most claim she is priceless.[2]

What would *Mona Lisa* be without its most famous detail? A big picture that never realized its potential.

In the same respect, your biggest and best intentions—for a relationship, for your followership, for a company or collaborative endeavor—will regularly fall short of their potential if your inspirational intentions do not translate into small acts of service and value.

"Most business people treat customer service like an ad campaign," said Scanlon. "They post it, promise it, and promote it. But unless they produce it in small increments every day, customer service is only lip service." It is *Mona Lisa* without the smile—a nice effort but not that different from anything, or anyone, else.

What you must always remember is that what motivates you to win friends is rarely what motivates others to grant you friendship.

You are motivated by what can be achieved with others' loyalty or support or collaborative effort. You are motivated by the big picture of connection and collaboration—by how things can be.

In contrast, those with whom you want to connect and collaborate see only the small pictures of their own experience with you. They see the true measure of your motives in bytes and feats. They are motivated by how things are.

Others are constantly asking of you: "How valuable is my relationship with this person?"

"What have you done for me lately?" still guides the mind of the masses, perhaps more so today amid the backdrop of millions of messages and messengers vying for attention. This does not suggest, as some believe, that you must continually outdo yourself or that you must parade as a spectacle. It simply means that the secret to all interpersonal progress is adding value, and doing so with regularity.

Unfortunately, "in the digital age winning friends has come to be about marketing, about standing out, about being significant," said legendary peak performance coach Tony Robbins in a recent interview. "There are two ways to be significant," he explained, "do something really well or do something really poorly. Unfortunately, infamy is the easiest way to get known today. Technology gives us the incredible power to connect with, learn from, and add value to any person on the planet 24/7, and yet we can burn someone or be foolish and get significance instantly. It is unfortunate many people choose that path."[3]

Besides the obvious relational consequences of this tack, the strategic problem is that there is no shortage of provocative items being broadcast in the digital age. Between media outlets, marketing campaigns. and me-first digital manners, your competition on the stage of sustaining interest is colossal. And the rewards are famously shallow.

The real key to winning friends and influencing people today, says Robbins, is "moving relationships from manipulative to meaningful. The only way you do that is by constantly adding meaning and value."

This is the scale on which every one of your interactions is judged—every tweet, post, email, call, and tangible encounter. To which side does your scale tip in each encounter—toward more value or less value? To which side does your scale tip over time? That is perhaps the more important question, because we all make mistakes. We have bad days. Still, the fallout of interpersonal failures can be swifter and more merciless than it has ever been before. For that reason alone, it is wisest to do everything within your power—through every medium and every message—to leave others a little better. While we certainly have some room for error, it's more of a laundry room than a grand ballroom. How many times has a mere glance put a relationship on the fritz?

Various traditions tell of gods and goddesses of justice. Themis, a Titan, was an organizer of communal affairs. Dike was the Greek goddess of justice, who weighed right and wrong. Justitia was the Roman personification of justice, forced to ascend to the heavens because of the wrongdoing of mortals. Ma'at was the Egyptian goddess who held the universe in order until the moment of creation and then became a heavenly regulator.

Out of these gods and goddesses arose a modern personification of Justice, the blindfolded, sword-holding, scale-bearing image associated with Western judicial systems. Her message couldn't be simpler: truth must be weighed on a case-by-case basis for truth to prevail.

A subtler message is this: anything can tip the scales. There isn't an idle argument or irrelevant fact in a case. The scales of justice measure it all.

What's true in justice holds true in human relationships. There are no neutral exchanges. You leave someone either a little better or a little worse.

Jordan was assessing his divorce a decade after it occurred, on the eve of his second wedding. A friend asked why his first one failed. It was, he said, because he neglected the scales. Every single interaction with his spouse sent her one of two messages— that she was the most important person in the world to him or that she wasn't. He'd sent the latter message far too often.

It is unrealistic to expect every exchange with every person to be life-altering. But your scale still tips one way or another every day. Knowing this should give you plenty of reasons to pay attention to every message you send. Placing this high a priority on altruism would set you apart in this digital age.

New York Times columnist David Brooks wrote a column called "High-Five Nation" in which he contrasted the humility on display after Japan's surrender at the end of World War II with what we see on display today. "On the day of victory, fascism had stood for grandiosity, pomposity, boasting and zeal. The allied propaganda mills had also produced their fair share of polemical excess. By 1945, everybody was sick of that. There was a mass hunger for a public style that was understated, self-abnegating, modest and spare."[4]

Humility, and the sense that others should occupy our minds as much as if not more than we do, was part of the culture of that era. Over time the sentiment began to change, writes Brooks. "Instead of being humble before God and history, moral salvation could be found through intimate contact with oneself . . . self-exposure and self-love became ways to win shares in the competition for attention."[5]

Certainly some people have gained attention today—perhaps "notoriety" is a better word—by worshipping themselves and creating a culture of celebrity around themselves. Some make millions off this strategy. But what is our impression of such people? Do they influence others for good? Perhaps after all the attention, they point people to a cultural good, which is better than nothing. But such people serve primarily as provocateurs. Like wine before a bland meal, they prepare our palate for nothing substantial.

There is one thing that hasn't changed over the millennia—something philosophers from every culture have concluded. It is as old as history itself. Zoroaster taught it to his followers in Persia 2,500 years ago. Confucius preached it in China 2,400 years ago. Lao-tse taught it to his disciples in the Valley of the Han. Buddha preached it on the bank of the holy Ganges around the same time. The sacred books of Hinduism taught it 1,000 years before that. They all concluded: Don't do to others what you wouldn't want them to do to you. Two thousand years ago Jesus put a slightly different spin on it: "Do to others what you would have them do to you."[6]

It is the only rule in human history we call golden.

An ironic advantage of our digital age is that many people hold a notion of superiority, which affords you a simple way to make a lasting impression: show them in some subtle way they are right. They are far more likely to return the favor.

"You know why I like you, Ike?" Winston Churchill asked President Dwight Eisenhower, who had labored, more or less harmoniously, alongside the strong personalities of Bernard Law Montgomery, Charles de Gaulle, and Franklin D. Roosevelt. "Because you ain't no glory hopper."[7]

Always leave people a little better, and you might be surprised how big it makes you and how far it takes you.

Part 3

How to Merit and Maintain Others' Trust

1

Avoid Arguments

In their book *The Preacher and the Presidents,* coauthors Nancy Gibbs and Michael Duffy detail the Reverend Billy Graham's path of unlikely ascendance and unmatched influence with not only seven U.S. presidents but also nearly every other global leader in the Western world. This path, they point out, was not without its resistance, especially early on. How Graham dealt with one of his staunchest opponents provides a preview of the first principle necessary for winning others' trust.

"In February 1954," they write, "Graham's patron Henry Luce wrote to *TIME*'s man in London, the legendary correspondent Andre Laguerre, to prepare him for what was about to come when Graham landed in London for a spring crusade." This was a time when church membership was much lower in Britain (between 5 and 15 percent of the population) than it was in the United States (59 percent). "'Religion in Britain is near death,' Luce noted, 'so Billy's impact will be worth watching. . . . Surely he will be scorned by all the people you know.'"

One of those scorners, explain Gibbs and Duffy, was a columnist from the *Daily Mirror,* "a man named William Connor, who called Graham 'Hollywood's version of John the Baptist.' As he often did with prominent critics, Graham suggested they meet in person; Connor mischievously suggested a rendezvous at a pub called the Baptist's Head."

As it turned out, neither Luce, Laguerre, nor Connor could estimate the effect Graham would have on the city. "So many people came the first week that from then on he held three meetings at Harringay Stadium on Saturdays. . . . Night after night eleven thousand people sat and another thousand stood, in rain or sleet or cold, to hear him preach." His audience included members of Parliament, an admiral, and the navy chief of staff. Nor could the journalists estimate the effect Graham would have on them personally—especially William Connor. After meeting the preacher for a chat at the irreverently named pub, Connor the critic became Connor the admirer.

"I never thought," he confessed of Graham in a subsequent column, "that friendliness had such a sharp cutting edge. I never thought that simplicity could cudgel us sinners so damned hard. We live and learn."[1]

While Graham can have employed a front of passive aggression by ignoring the cheeky jabs, or fought the jabs with press-worthy indignation, he chose a higher road, a far more effective path. He avoided an argument altogether and won his critic over with grace and goodwill.

Arguing with another person will rarely get you anywhere; they usually end with each person more firmly convinced of his rightness. You may be right, dead right, but arguing is just as futile as if you were dead wrong.

Humorist Dave Barry made this point quite well when he said: "I argue very well. Ask any of my remaining friends. I can win an argument on any topic, against any opponent. People know this, and steer clear of me at parties. Often, as a sign of their great respect, they don't even invite me."

So much of our time online is spent arguing or feeding arguments. Look no further than comments at the bottom of popular blogs and news sites. It's nearly always a string of he said/she said or attempts at one-upmanship. Beyond that, the recent and ongoing corporate and political banter seems to primarily involve proving points and stating cases instead of finding common ground on which to build something of mutual value. Few of these arguments change people's minds. Because the arguments are digitally veiled and lack the clear-cut consequences of tangible confrontations, both parties can get away with devolving into snarky personal attacks and passive ambiguity—the least effective tools of human relations.

Such was the case when former BP chief executive Tony Hayward took a hard line of personal self-exoneration and arrogant apathy in reaction to the tragic *Deepwater Horizon* explosion and subsequent oil spill that took eleven human lives, ravaged the Gulf states ecosystem, and devastated the livelihood of thousands more workers around the country.

According to an article in *The Times,* he started by refuting scientific findings about the nature and amount of the spill. Then his contention that the spill was "tiny" compared to the size of the ocean and that the environmental impact of America's biggest oil spill, and of the 950,000 gallons of toxic dispersant that have been used to treat it, would be "very, very modest" set off a series of gaffes from which he could not recover, including a backhanded apology to the people of Louisiana in which he stated, "I would like my life back."[2]

When, two days after dodging questions and ditching blame before U.S. lawmakers, he was found in Cowes on the southern coast of England for a yacht race in which his boat, *Bob,* was entered, it merely highlighted what had already been established: whether or not he was right, Hayward had lost both his credibility and his case in the court of public opinion. When influence and impact are at stake, it is often the only court that matters.[3]

After his line of argument, few could trust the man. He seemed to care about two things and two things only: himself and his empire. Under his argumentative approach, BP quickly went from suspect to reject, regardless of what story the facts would turn out to tell. Wherever BP was sold to consumers, boycotting began. Why fill up at a BP station when there were a dozen others belonging to companies that didn't have fearlessly uncaring leaders trying to argue their way to exoneration?

Some of the chain of reaction was based on perception, of course, but reality remains perception when the facts aren't clear. And when the case is in the realm of human relations, perception is often so strong that even irrefutable facts are not enough to supplant the wave of bad press that preceded them.

In Hayward's defense, after his dismissal from BP—a day he called one of the saddest of his life—he was far more empathetic not only about his company's role in the spill but also about his approach to the tragedy. Friends laud Hayward as a kind and generous family man, and there is no doubt they have good reason. Furthermore, BP has been a solid, respectable company for decades. Both deserve to be valued for their finest moments, no less than any of us would had our argumentative approach with a spouse, colleague, or client been widely publicized. And both Hayward and BP still likely will. But why not avoid the valleys in the first place?

We will face conflict nearly every day of our lives. So how do we prevent a tactful discussion from becoming an aggressive argument? In the end you must value interdependence higher than independence and understand that deferential negotiation is more effective in the long run than a noncompliant crusade.

One South American leader has proven this principle's merit

despite great historical and personal odds. For a man who came from poverty, who led a labor union in a country not known for workers' rights, who watched his wife die when she was eight months pregnant because they couldn't afford adequate health care, and who formed his own political party, one might expect a fighter. But Luiz Inácio Lula de Silva, called Lula by all, defied expectations at every turn.

"My mother always said two people can't fight if one person doesn't want to," Lula told a reporter once. And so Lula doesn't fight, an approach that helped him become the president of Brazil and hold the position for almost ten years. When his newly formed socialist party lost elections year after year, he developed an alliance with a right-wing party and courted business leaders despite his social goals. When he became president on the promise to prioritize the impoverished in Brazil, he also built alliances with Brazil's wealthy and vast upper class by focusing on growing the economy.

"I consider myself a negotiator. If we want peace and democracy, we have to be tolerant, to negotiate more," he has said.[4] Lula's tolerance and negotiation helped him achieve astounding things during his time in office. Through building alliances both domestically and internationally, he enacted social programs that pulled more than twenty million people out of poverty and into the middle class, while also creating a period of strong economic growth and stability. In a country known for the vast divide between the rich and the poor, Lula's people skills put Brazil on course to reverse historical inequalities.[5]

The notion of communication has been greatly misinterpreted, explains corporate behavioral specialist Esther Jeles. "We have come to believe it is all about the delivery. In doing so, we regularly forfeit the full potential [of] our exchanges."[6]

Jeles reminds the executives and employees of corporate

clients such as Twentieth Century Fox, Leo Burnett, and Harpo, Inc., that there is an important reason all personal growth techniques spring from the act of listening to your inner wisdom. Inside us all is "a vault of better self-understanding, higher knowledge and greater ideas," she explains. "Tension and conflict occur when you—and/or those with you—discard the notion that others also have inner wisdom that ought to be heard."

How, then, do we build a practice of avoiding arguments? See the singular advantage of operating interdependently.

This occurs, says Jeles, when you "acknowledge that greater interpersonal results are always more probable when your experience and insight are compounded with that of others."

No matter how expressive or persuasive you might be, this does not occur by one person trumping another. It occurs when the end result of the tension is a mutual stretching of insight and personal growth. And if you can see your interactions clearly despite tension and conflict, there is little you can't accomplish in collaboration with others.

"All of us know how to get attention," asserts Jeles, "but few of us know how to get attention and respect at the same time." Set yourself apart by being one who avoids the arguments that most jump into with both feet.

2

Never Say, "You're Wrong"

The best solution, wisest decision, and brightest idea nearly always exist outside of what one party brings to the table. Yet we find it quite easy to declare another person wrong, often before we've taken the time to consider what he or she is saying.

Even when we believe another is wrong, there is only one way to guarantee an unenviable end to an interaction and all chance of connection or meaningful collaboration, and that is to tell the other person we think so.

"Those who forget the past are condemned to repeat it. Those who learn the wrong lessons from the past may be equally doomed," writes Harvard Business School professor and coauthor of *Negotiation Genius,* Deepak Malhotra, in the opening of a Forbes.com article comparing the 2011 NFL revenue share dispute with a similar dispute between the owners and players of the National Hockey League in 2004–5.

In both disputes, the owners, concerned about rising costs, asked the players to accept a smaller share of league revenues. In both disputes, the players rejected the owners' request and asked to see proof of the rising costs. In both disputes, the owners initially refused to substantiate their claims. In the NHL the situation turned dire because neither would back down. "Accusations of greed were rampant," explains Malhotra. "Unable to bridge the divide even months after the collective bargaining agreement . . . had expired, the NHL eventually canceled the season. Two billion dollars in revenues were lost."

Was the result a foregone conclusion? According to Malhotra, it was avoidable if only the sides had understood the basic human relations problem at the heart of the matter. "Both sides lost the season because the owners refused to acknowledge that players had legitimate concerns. By seeing them as greedy rather than mistrusting, the owners adopted the wrong strategy—intransigence rather than transparency—for too long."

The dispute fell into the trap of "I'm right, you're wrong" because neither would consider the alternative: that perhaps both were right. There is a critical lesson here. "Negotiations become more productive," concludes Malhotra, "when each party acknowledges that the other may have legitimate concerns. In the NFL dispute, both the owners and the players need to bring a more nuanced perspective to the bargaining table—or fans across America may be doing something other than watching pro football games next fall."[1]

Nuance, or subtle difference, is a critical concept to remember in the midst of disagreement. In most disputes, our differences with others are far subtler than we allow ourselves to see. We so easily treat dissonance like a chasm that cannot be crossed—the only resolution being one party taking a dive (or being shoved) off the cliff, so that only one party remains. It's far from the truth. "Friendship that insists upon agreement on all matters is not worth the name," exhorted Mahatma Gandhi. "Friendship to be real must ever sustain the weight of honest differences, however sharp they be."[2] The truth is that disagreement is more often a small crack in the sidewalk that can easily be negotiated if we come to the discussion table with a more open mind.

"We talk because we know something," explained corporate

behavioral specialist Esther Jeles in a recent interview. "Or we think we know something. Or, in the workplace, because there is an expectation that we 'should' know something."[3] This expectation of knowledge tends to work against us in interactions because it closes off our minds to the possibilities that exist outside the knowledge we bring to the table. We enter interactions with corroboration in mind, and if that corroboration does not come, we spend the remainder of the interaction attempting to either rebut the other's assessment or rebuke the other's right to make an assessment in the first place. The result is that collaboration—or the possibility of it—is forfeited. If that's your approach, you will rarely progress far in relationships.

All effective problem solving, collaboration, and dispute resolution, said Jeles, begins with an emptying of the mind—of what we know or what we think we should know.

"This can feel incredibly unnatural," she admitted, "because we have been trained to demonstrate what we think, to show our knowledge, our smarts—we think therefore we talk." Yet by approaching a conversation with a blank slate, we take a humbler and more honest approach. We acknowledge the possibility that we may not know all the facts and that we may not in fact be the only one who is right. Better yet, we create the possibility for meaningful collaboration—the melting of thoughts, ideas, and experiences into something greater than the sum of two parties.

The notion that we might not be the only one who is right and that we may in fact also be wrong is of course nearly always the case, but we seem so averse to admitting it. Why is that?

More often than not it is because we value personal victory over collaborative possibility. Yet in doing so, we not only stunt the relationship, we also punt the probability of greater progress than we originally considered. We expect too little if in the midst of disagreement we only seek a winner.

Jeles shared the following story from her experience with

a well-known media conglomerate whose swift response to a national disaster caused an aftermath of in-house conflict.

Her cell rang at midnight—it was the president of a media conglomerate that had retained her. The man needed Jeles to facilitate a meeting first thing in the morning to deal with an assembly line of catastrophes.

The president was referring to the Hurricane Katrina tragedy. In the wake of one of the United States' worst natural disasters, his company had swiftly deployed 90 percent of its employees to various regions of the Gulf Coast. No planning, no strategy, just some general instructions to come back with the important stories. Now, two weeks later, the teams had returned to the realities of resuming business in the severely disjointed aftermath.

"I have four production teams fighting about whose coverage should take priority," the president explained. "I have legal fighting with production about waiting for proper vetting. And I have accounting fighting with everyone about divvying up the huge expense of the whole thing." He paused briefly, then went on to tell her how much it had cost: "Six times more than any previous production."

Jeles's role, said the president, was to meet with all the bickering leadership teams and help them talk it out.

Jeles knew precisely what to do.

The next morning, as she sat in the auditorium where the meeting was to be held, she watched a familiar sight: the executives and their senior staff each entered the auditorium metaphorically carrying a case—the case they would state to win the dispute. As they settled into their seats, she jumped in with an invitation.

"I would like everyone to take a moment and ask yourself this question: 'What could I have done differently during this assignment that would have helped the other departments succeed?'"

In her head, Jeles says, she could hear a series of thuds as the talking heads dropped their verbal cases to the floor. Ears then perked up around the room as, one by one, the team leaders shared their "in the future we could . . ." thoughts.

The CFO began by suggesting that his accounting and production teams could lay out a preliminary budget for projects.

"We don't have time," the executive vice president of production barked back, "for sitting around and making budgets when a story is breaking."

Jeles intervened with a question: "Can you see why accounting is suggesting this practice?"

"So we don't overspend," the executive vice president replied.

"Accounting," Jeles added, "has an imperative function for the survival of this company, equally as important as production." She then asked the chief financial officer and the executive vice president of production, "Could your two departments collaborate on creating a preliminary budget for weekly assignments and a breaking news budget with moving caps based on crisis proportions?"

Both nodded. The mediation moved on.

The company's chief counsel suggested legal could compose a "most common vetting problems" document so production would know beforehand how to avoid long vetting processes.

Jeles looked at the executive vice president, who was nodding. "That would be very helpful," she agreed.

"Done," replied the chief counsel.

The meeting continued in this manner, even going so far as to roll out the specifics of suggested items including budgets and documents. Within thirty minutes, everyone in the room was in agreement about the solutions. The meeting was formally adjourned, and it was then that perhaps the most surprising thing of all happened: many executives and their staff stayed behind to capitalize on the collaboration momentum.

As Jeles picked up her bag to leave, the president approached. "In twenty-five years," he asserted, "I have never attended a meeting where there were more people listening than talking."

In the spirit of all great artisans who begin with only a blank page, white canvas, or lump of clay, we must enter all disputes with a mind open to what more we might discover and produce together. Only then can our true interpersonal potential be tapped.

On June 26, 2000, in the White House's East Room, where Teddy Roosevelt used to box, where Amy Carter had her high school prom, and where Lewis and Clark once camped in their tents, President Bill Clinton announced the completion of the first survey of the entire human genome. "Humankind is on the verge of gaining immense, new power to heal," he remarked.[4]

Next to him stood Dr. Francis Collins, noted geneticist and the head of the Human Genome Project. For seven years he had led an international team of more than a thousand scientists in what *Time* journalist J. Madeleine Nash called "the challenge of pulling off a technological tour de force that many ranked alongside splitting the atom and landing men on the moon. 'There is only one human genome project, and it will happen only once,' Collins said at the time. 'The chance to stand at the helm of that project and put my own personal stamp on it is more than I could imagine.'"[5]

That Collins had to do it while competing against a former colleague made it all the more interesting.

In May 1998, five years after Collins agreed to helm the project, Craig Venter, a passionate NIH biologist who was among the countless scientists dedicated to harnessing genomes to cure diseases, announced he was founding a company to scoop Collins's project by four years.

The "race" between Collins and Venter made for great press. Central to ongoing commentary were the two men's very different personalities—one brash, one reserved. And Collins, the reserved one, had little choice but to compete. Doing so meant getting scientists from six countries, numerous government agencies, and many more numerous university labs to work together for a common interest rather than individual glory.

So it was even more remarkable that in the East Room that day Francis Collins introduced Craig Venter this way: "Articulate, provocative and never complacent, he has ushered in a new way of thinking about biology. . . . It is an honor and a pleasure to invite him to tell you about this landmark achievement."

Collins chose a path of cooperation and partnership and resisted the temptation to proclaim Venter wrong. Ultimately, he merely saw him as different. But different didn't have to mean opposed. While Collins admits the two are "different people . . . wired in a different way," *Time*'s Nash points out, "Collins now says that he considers Venter to have 'been a stimulant in a very positive way.'"

At the heart of the assertion that others are wrong is actually an unspoken admittance that we don't want to be rejected. It is in the spirit of not wanting to be wrong ourselves that we project that role on others. If not for a pointed patent leather reminder, Dale Carnegie himself would have fallen prey to this unenviable reaction.

Shortly after the close of World War I, he was the business manager for Sir Ross Smith. During the war, Sir Ross had been the Australian ace out in Palestine; shortly after peace was declared, he astonished the world by flying halfway around it in thirty days. No such feat had ever been attempted before. It created a tremendous sensation. The Australian government awarded him fifty thousand dollars, the king of England knighted him, and for a while he was the talk of the global town.

Carnegie was attending a banquet one night given in Sir

Ross's honor, and during the dinner, the man sitting next to him told a humorous story that hinged on the quotation "There's a divinity that shapes our ends, rough-hew them how we will."

The raconteur mentioned that the quotation was from the Bible. He was wrong, and Carnegie knew it positively. By his own admission, he appointed himself as an unsolicited and unwelcome committee of one to correct the storyteller.

The other man stuck to his guns. From Shakespeare? Absurd! That quotation was from the Bible. And the man knew it.

Frank Gammond, an old friend of Carnegie's, was seated to his left. Gammond had devoted years to the study of Shakespeare. So the storyteller and Carnegie agreed to submit the question to the expert.

Mr. Gammond listened, kicked Carnegie under the table, and then said, "Dale, you are wrong. The gentleman is right. It is from the Bible."

On their way home that night, Carnegie said to Mr. Gammond, "Frank, you knew that quotation was from Shakespeare."

"Yes, of course," he replied, "Hamlet, act five, scene two. But we were guests at a festive occasion, my dear Dale. Why prove to a man he is wrong? Is that going to make him like you? Why not let him save his face? He didn't ask for your opinion. He didn't want it. Always avoid the acute angle."

It taught Carnegie a lesson he never forgot.

Telling people they are wrong will only earn you enemies. Few people respond logically when they are told they are wrong; most respond emotionally and defensively because you are questioning their judgment. You shouldn't just avoid the words "You're wrong." You can tell people they are wrong by a look or an intonation or a gesture, so you must guard against showing judgment in all of the ways that you communicate. And if you are going to prove anything, don't let anybody know it.

It is easy to allow a certain tone to creep into our online communication, a tone that tells another person that we believe he or she is wrong. Sometimes we don't even realize the tone is there until we read what we've written sometime later. We believe we are being diplomatic, but each word, presented in absence of expression or a soft tone of voice, is usually a condemnation. This is one of the reasons settling disputes is best accomplished in person.

Instead of presenting a truncated argument through email, IM, or Twitter, create a more respectful, conciliatory environment for conversation. Then offer your point with an open mind. While you in fact might be right and the other person wrong, there is no sense in denting a person's ego or permanently damaging a relationship. If you remember those who obstinately insisted you were wrong, you can be certain others will remember you in that same negative light if you choose to turn an interaction into an opportunity to teach a lesson instead of a chance to strengthen a relationship.

Always default to diplomacy. Admit that you may be wrong. Concede that the other person may be right. Be agreeable. Ask questions. And above all, consider the situation from the other's perspective and show that person respect.

Such a humble approach leads to unexpected relationships, unexpected collaboration, and unexpected results.

3

Admit Faults Quickly and Emphatically

Only slightly less of a cliché than "The check is in the mail" is this: "The ref blew the call." While the sport and circumstances vary, referees regularly make mistakes. Occasionally the consequences are significant. Around the world some are so famous they have their own monikers.

Take the "hand of God" goal, for instance. In the 1986 World Cup quarterfinals, Argentina and England were locked in a scoreless tie when Argentina's captain, Diego Maradona, leapt high in the air over goalie Peter Shilton and punched the ball into the net. The referee, Ali Bin Nasser, didn't see the handball and ruled the goal legal.

Then there was Jeffrey Maier. In the 1996 American League Championship Series, the Orioles led the Yankees 4–3 in the bottom of the eighth inning when Yankees shortstop Derek Jeter hit a long fly ball into right field. The twelve-year-old Maier reached over the wall and caught the ball, preventing Orioles right fielder Tony Tarasco from making the play. Umpire Rich Garcia improperly called a home run instead of an out or automatic double. The Yankees went on to win the game.

Add to these incidents ten thousand other blown calls, and fan exasperation at referee errors can be faintly understood. Certainly we are passionate about our teams. But referees are human, after all, and we can understand making mistakes. What makes exasperation linger, however, is the inability or unwillingness of the referees to admit their mistakes.

That is what makes one of the worst examples of referee error so extraordinary—and ultimately redeeming.

It's been called the "perfect game robbery." Since 1900—the generally recognized start of baseball's modern era—nearly four hundred thousand games have been played in the United States. During this span only eighteen times has a pitcher delivered perfection, retiring every opposing batter in order without giving up a walk or a hit and without his teammates putting a runner on base with an error. To put this in perspective, the odds of a perfect game being thrown in baseball (one in twenty thousand) are far smaller than the chance you will be struck by lightning in your lifetime.[1]

But a perfect game is precisely what Detroit Tigers pitcher Armando Galarraga had happening one early June evening in 2010. He'd recorded twenty-six consecutive outs and had gotten the twenty-seventh batter to tap a weak ground ball to the first baseman. Galarraga ran from the mound, took the throw from the first baseman, tagged the bag ahead of the runner and got ready to celebrate. There was only one problem: the umpire, Jim Joyce, swung his arms wide and shouted, "Safe!"

Galarraga's perfect game had been lost in one of the most egregious blown calls in sports history.

But here is where things took an equally unexpected turn. It is perhaps the most significant and memorable detail of the story.

When he got back to the umpire's locker room, Joyce immediately cued the game video and watched the play—only once. He saw how badly he'd blown the call. But instead of letting the dust settle in silence like so many of his colleagues, Joyce chose a different path. He walked straight to the Detroit Tigers locker room and requested an audience with Galarraga.

Face red as a tomato, tears in his eyes, he hugged Galarraga and managed to get out two words before dissolving into tears: "Lo siento."

He apologized boldly and unreservedly. In doing so he changed sports history. There had been previous perfect games in baseball, but this was the first redemption game.

There are many things that are common to us all—birth, death, and a lifetime full of mistakes, errors, and gaffes. We all know this, and the vast majority of our mistakes, while temporarily frustrating and even maddening to others, are forgivable.

Why, then, do we have such a hard time admitting them?

Take Tiger Woods, for example. His Thanksgiving-night car crash outside his home quickly triggered seemingly endless accusations and allegations of extramarital affairs. Where once rumors of affairs would be passed around town as unsubstantiated gossip, our digital age can broadcast, accuse, and convict almost overnight.

Woods's response? A prepared, vague admission of his "transgressions" and a request for privacy. His professional and personal world soon collapsed around him. Sponsors dropped him, his wife left him, and his golf skills suffered greatly.

Could he have taken a different road? Of course.

In the first weeks of the breaking news, before the fallout of endorsement deals being cancelled or Woods's wife's departure, PR experts pointed to a different approach that could have stopped the bleeding much sooner. In a *Phoenix Business Journal* article, journalist Mike Sunnucks cited Abbie Fink of HMA Public Relations:

> Fink said Woods and his camp chose silence over getting in front of a story that ended up being driven by TMZ and the *National Enquirer.* "In the absence of anything coming from Tiger, the media will go find the sources elsewhere. And after today's news, it would appear that there are plenty of people willing to share their side of the story," Fink said.
>
> Troy Corder, a principal with Critical Public Relations in Phoenix, said the Woods camp made numerous mistakes including essentially lying, hunkering down with a bunker mentality and not being ready to respond to tabloid reports, which have been true in part.[2]

A sincere and swift apology, publicly made, would have brought him to earth in the right sort of way. He had been an untouchable icon. A quick and emphatic admission not only would have cleared the air but also would have confirmed to people he was like all of us, human, mistake-prone, and messy— something we all knew anyway. That would have only helped him return to others' good graces much sooner.

Digital Royalty CEO Amy Martin observed at the time:

> Tiger should humanize his brand via social media outlets, specifically with Twitter and real-time raw video. His Facebook presence has a polished and promotional tonality leaving fans wanting a glimpse behind-the-scenes. . . . If he had allowed people to see the person behind the superstar personality, perceptions and expectations could have been different in recent events.[3]

Unfortunately, it was not the road Tiger's team chose after the events that changed the course of his career. And the dust took much longer to settle. Such is the effect of ignoring this principle in the digital age. Negative news spreads faster than ever. If you've made a mistake, it is far better that you control the news being spread. Come clean quickly and convincingly.

One reason we find it so difficult to admit our faults is that we are inclined to forget the messages that apologies bear. This forgetfulness is all the more dangerous today. If we admit our faults immediately and emphatically, it is like shooting a full-page press release across the wires that confirms we genuinely care about the people we hurt, that we are humbled, and that we want to make things right. People rarely hold on to anger and disappointment when they can see that we view ourselves and the situation properly. We are much more forgiving of those who are willing to come clean right away.

Contrast the public's view today of baseball slugger Jason Giambi, who immediately and tearfully admitted steroid use as the scandal was coming to light, against former slugger Mark McGwire, who waited five years to clear the air. Giambi had his life back rather quickly. The public was gracious and quick to forgive. While McGwire certainly had his reasons for delaying his explanation, in many baseball fans' minds he forever wears a scarlet S on his chest. A half decade after his stellar career ended, he still remained a long way off from receiving the Hall of Fame induction that was once a foregone conclusion.

If we are aloof and ambiguous about our mistakes, we also shoot out a full-page press release, but one that reads: "I would like my life back." While we'd all like our pre-mistake lives back after a mistake has been made, we have to remember that no one changed the circumstances but us. It is not others' duty to give us back the life we took from ourselves. Only we can get our life back. That always begins with admitting our faults quickly and emphatically.

What all of us at one time or another forget is that there is a certain degree of satisfaction in having the courage to admit one's errors. It not only clears the air of guilt and defensiveness but also often helps solve the problem created by the error much quicker.

Ronald Reagan was known as the "Great Communicator" because, to the joy of his supporters and the consternation of his critics, he could move from a place of defensive weakness to undeniable strength with a simple quip.

One of his tried-and-true methods? An easy familiarity with the apology. During one particularly rocky patch of his presidency, he poked fun at his own White House, conceding, "Our right hand doesn't know what our far right hand is doing."[4]

Reagan knew it was easier to bear self-condemnation than condemnation from others. If we know we are going to be rebuked anyhow, isn't it better to beat the other person to the punch?

When we recognize and admit our errors, the response from others is typically forgiveness and generosity. Quickly the error is diminished in their eyes. It is only when we shirk responsibility or refuse to admit our errors immediately that we raise the ire of those around us and the original misjudgment seems to grow in importance and negative effect.

Today we have the opportunity to broadcast our apologies, to let everyone involved know we made an error and are sorry for it. We nip negative opinions in the bud when we take that action. And we gain people's respect, because it takes courage to admit our faults publicly.

It also takes courage to admit our faults privately. Consider our families. How hard is it for husbands and wives to admit their mistakes to each other? It's akin to stabbing yourself in the gut. But no matter what that mistake may have been, it is crucial to choose the path of humility and rely on the power of forgiveness.

Anne was a successful finance executive and mother of three. Honors graduate of an Ivy League school, she'd never really failed at anything. She married the man of her dreams and then one night found herself hanging out with some of her buddies from work while at an out-of-town convention. One drink led to two, and two to four, and the group of buddies got smaller until it was just a male coworker and her.

They decided to leave the bar, and in the elevator they kissed. A few more floors and footsteps later and they stood outside her hotel room door. She opened it. They kissed again. Then they stopped. He backed away and so did she.

Each was married; they loved their spouses. They kissed again. And then they stopped, and he left and the door closed behind him. Anne went to bed alone . . . and then woke up to the nightmare that she'd betrayed the man of her dreams.

She went home two days later and said nothing for six years. It was a mistake. A one-time mistake with only one witness, who wasn't going to say anything either.

The years passed with the memory locked away in a mental and emotional safe. She knew that if this secret got out, it would be the end of her life as the one who had it all together, the one who made no mistakes.

But one evening, while on vacation, she told her husband everything. He looked at her and started crying. Of all the reactions she'd considered, that hadn't been one of them.

Over the next several weeks, they talked to each other, to

their friends, and to their pastor. Her husband grieved, and with every minute of his grief her own heart broke. But something else broke as well—her mask of perfectionism. As friends learned of her mistake, she was overwhelmed by the very thing she never considered possible—grace and forgiveness.

She discovered that the truth did indeed have the power to set her free. Anne's mistake was not without consequence, but in admitting the mistake and seeking forgiveness, she allowed room for a different perspective on her life, a perspective in which she was safe being imperfect. If only she had given herself room six years sooner.

The same perspective exists for us all if we are brave enough to own it. Any fool can defend a mistake—and most fools do—but admitting your mistake raises you above the pack and gives you a feeling of exultation.

At the end of 2010, people in the sports world engaged in that casual end-of-year discussion about whom *Sports Illustrated* would name as its "Sportsman of the Year." The honor ended up going to New Orleans Saints quarterback Drew Brees for leading the once hapless Saints to their first-ever Super Bowl victory. It was a fitting selection.

But Chris Harry of AOLnews.com believed two different men should have shared the prize instead. "As far as sheer sportsmanship, to me, nothing compared to the fallout from the night of June 3." Harry goes on to recount the now-famous story of the blown perfect game and concludes:

> About 16 hours later, the Tigers and Indians played again, but the meeting that mattered came before the game when Galarraga was tabbed for the trip to home plate to turn in the lineup card. Joyce was waiting for him. The two exchanged handshakes and hugs in one of the most inspiring, emotional

and moving displays of sportsmanship any sport had ever seen. It was a moment worthy of being relived and helped us learn a lesson about invoking class and dignity when circumstances very easily—especially in this day and age—could have brought about a very different reaction.[5]

Oh, the power of two words to change everything: "Lo siento. I'm sorry."

4
—

Begin in a Friendly Way

"**S**uccessful leaders . . . are always initiators," writes leadership expert John C. Maxwell in his flagship book *The 21 Irrefutable Laws of Leadership*. He then recalls an instance where beginning in a friendly way was not only necessary but highly recommended. Still a young man, he had been hired to take over the leadership of a troubled church in Lancaster, Ohio, where he was told a large and intimidating man named Jim Butz, the elected lay leader of the congregation, was the most influential person in the organization. He was also told Jim had a reputation for maverick behavior that at times had led the church down the wrong path.

The first thing Maxwell did was arrange a meeting with Jim in his office. It could have been an awkward or even grossly misperceived moment—a twenty-five-year-old rookie summoning the sixty-five-year-old patriarch to meet with him—but Maxwell dispelled that notion immediately. The second Jim sat down, Maxwell began with a humble acknowledgment of the situation. Jim was the influencer in the church, and Maxwell wanted to work with him, not against him. Maxwell then suggested they meet once a week for lunch to talk through the issues and make decisions together. "While I'm the leader here," said Maxwell, "I'll never take any decision to the people without first discussing it with you. I really want to work with you. . . . We can do a lot of great thing together at this church, but the decision is yours."

When he finished, Maxwell explains, "Jim didn't say a word. He got up from his seat, walked into the hall, and stopped to take a drink at the water fountain. I followed him out and waited. After a long time, he stood up straight and turned around. . . . I could see that tears were rolling down his cheeks. And then he gave me a great big bear hug and said, 'You can count on me to be on your side.'"[1]

Friendliness begets friendliness. We are more inclined to agree with another person or see things from his perspective when we have friendly feelings toward him. If, in contrast, we feel a person is busy or brusque or uninterested in sharing a common courtesy, we tend to mirror the sentiment. This is a difficult obstacle to overcome whether you've just met the person or have known him awhile.

Where the initiation of interactions is concerned, no approach sets the tone more effectively than gentleness and affability, even if the other person is a source of pain, frustration, or anger. A friendly greeting says: "You are worth my time. You are valuable." This subtle message has tremendous power—more than most realize.

In *The Seven Arts of Change,* author David Shaner shares an incredible experience that taught him the immense power of beginning in a friendly way.[2] He had been recruited by a longtime friend to teach Ki-Aikido at the Aspen-Snowmass Academy of Martial Arts, just up the road from Pitkin County, a Colorado locale made famous in 1970 when American journalist Hunter S. Thompson ran for sheriff on the "Freak Ticket," promoting the decriminalization of drugs for personal use, turning asphalt streets into grassy meadows, banning buildings that obscured the mountain view, and renaming Aspen "Fat City" to deter investors. Thompson narrowly lost the election that year, but his sentiment set the stage for another, less controversial, but equally unconventional man to become sheriff. His name was Dick Kienast, whose campaign poster had cited Sissela Bok's vision of societal values: "Trust is a social good to be protected just as much as the air we breathe or the water we drink."[3]

Kienast believed civility and compassion should rule all law enforcement interaction whether it involved violent felons or frustrated traffic offenders. "It was a momentous change initiative," writes Shaner, "and one that many thought foolish and unnecessary. . . . Nevertheless, he moved forward in confidence." Among Shaner's first Ki-Aikido students at Aspen-Snowmass Academy were Sheriff Kienast and his deputies. Bob Braudis was one of Kienast's key deputies and would go on to succeed him as Pitkin County sheriff. Before then Deputy Braudis would establish his legacy with a compelling display of beginning in a friendly way.

Braudis was an imposing presence and fit the stereotype of a brawny, no-nonsense cop. This presence served as a stark and effective contrast to his demeanor with people. He never raised his voice, even in the midst of volatile situations. One event serves as a case in point.

While Deputy Braudis was the patrol director, a dispatch came through that an armed man was holding all the patrons hostage at a local restaurant called the Woody Creek Tavern. Braudis was the first to arrive on the scene, and from outside the building he was apprised of the situation. The man's estranged wife was prohibiting him from visiting his daughter, whom he had seen in the restaurant. Rather than attempting a peaceful greeting, something clicked inside the man. He yanked out a gun and forced everyone inside to comply with his wishes.

Deputy Braudis assessed the danger and took a different tack. He peacefully approached the window unarmed. Sensing the deputy's affability, the gunman allowed him to enter the building. Braudis then proceeded to address the man in a civil manner, asking him to consider the consequences of his actions, which could ultimately lead to him never seeing his daughter again.

"Bob's placid demeanor, his rational discussion of the real issues, and his empathy toward the man's rage validated the suspect," writes Shaner. "And the more the man talked with Bob, the more he realized that much of his anger was with himself. He eventually put down his weapon. The man's whole demeanor then changed. . . . Bob explained that exiting the tavern with cuffs on would put all the law enforcement people outside the tavern at ease so that neither Bob nor the suspect would run the risk of being shot. The man complied, and the conflict was ended peacefully."[4]

Consider this story the next time you sit down to write an email to somebody who has made you frustrated or angry. Will you begin with a civil, courteous tone or let your emotions take over and jump into conflict? Will you take a few moments to inquire about the other person's life or work situation or to create a bond through some shared interest by telling them something about yourself? If you begin in a friendly manner, you are far more likely to get the positive results you seek, especially if you and the other person are currently at odds.

"I do not like that man," Abraham Lincoln once said. "I must get to know him better."[5]

If you believe building a friendly rapport will be critical to achieving a certain outcome, using texts, chats, or other short forms of communication isn't likely to get you very far. Because of the limited space and the lack of intonation and nonverbal cues to support your sentiment, it's very difficult to create the level of communication necessary to convey affability. If face-to-face is not possible, at least use a medium that will allow time and space to convey a level of friendliness that in Carnegie's time ruled human relations. It takes creativity and a bit more time to replicate the effect of a warm smile and a firm handshake, but it can be done.

"Social media requires that business leaders start thinking like small-town shop owners," concurs entrepreneur Gary Vaynerchuk, who wrote *The Thank You Economy*.

> This means taking the long view and avoiding short-term benchmarks to gauge progress. . . . In short, business leaders are going to have to relearn the ethics and skills our great-grandparents' generation used in building their own businesses and took for granted. . . . [O]nly the companies that can figure out how to mind their manners in a very old-fashioned way—and do it authentically—are going to have a prayer of competing.[6]

There was an age when people left their houses in their best attire and said hello to all they passed on the way to work, when a meeting meant meeting and when a call meant paying someone a visit rather than using the phone. While our transactions span the globe today, making such tangible connection more infrequent, it is still key to treat others in the same spirit you would if they were before you. Of his growing wine empire, Vaynerchuk explains, "We talk to every single individual as though we're going to be sitting next to that person at his or her mother's house that night for dinner."[7] It's the proper perspective because it places the burden of accountability squarely where it should be—on the messenger's shoulders.

The mistake many make today is placing the burden of accountability on the recipient of the message. We use the responses and reactions of others as the only gauge of whether we have taken the right approach or made the right impression. This is a slippery slope on two fronts.

First, it can lead to laziness in considering motive's role in effective connection. If garnering a great response is the only measure of connection, then we easily become mere entertainers, provocateurs, and product pimps who think only about the next great gimmick to grab people's interest. Shock value is worth little where true connection is concerned.

Second, responses can be deceptive, especially in the beginning. A tweet may garner many retweets, but this does not mean that those relaying your message to others have become fans or even friends. They may be thinking of someone else who might benefit from the message or might want to consider the product; worse, they may have in mind someone who would laugh alongside the retweeter at your lack of knowledge, sincerity, or tact. An online marketing campaign might generate a spike in site traffic or a print media campaign lots of journalistic buzz, but wise businesspeople know this does not mean relationships are being formed.

There is a big difference between engagement and interest. Interest is piqued in a number of ways, many of which are less than genial. It often begins and ends on a superficial level because the primary emotions tapped are curiosity, surprise, or disgust.

Engagement occurs on a deeper level when a person's core values are tapped. Common to all core values is the notion of being considered worthy of relationship. When you engage another in a friendly manner, you convey to him he is someone worthy of friendship, someone whom you'd like to call friend. It is for this reason "he who sows courtesy reaps friendship."[8]

If you want your voice to reach through the noise and beneath the surface to others' motives for moving in your direction, begin in a friendly way. The first impression that makes is far more memorable than anything the loudest or most provocative attention-grabber on the planet could come up with.

Years ago, when Carnegie was a barefoot boy walking through the woods to a country school in northwest Missouri, he read a fable about the sun and the wind. It serves as a vivid reminder of the power of this principle of earning others' trust.

The sun and wind debated about which was the stronger, and the wind said, "I'll prove I am. See the old man down there with a coat? I bet I can get his coat off him quicker than you can."

So the sun went behind a cloud, and the wind blew until it was almost a tornado, but the harder it blew, the tighter the old man clutched his coat to him.

Finally the wind calmed down and gave up, and then the sun came out from behind the clouds and smiled kindly on the old man. Presently, the man mopped his brow and pulled off his coat. The sun then reminded the wind that gentleness and friendliness were always stronger than fury and force.

It's a timely lesson in an age that appears to divvy rewards based on greatest volume, speed, and splash. Such rewards mean little in the long run because engagement that engenders longevity is continually authenticated on mutual benefit and trust. If you don't establish a foundation for both from the beginning through a friendly sentiment, both become more difficult to secure with each passing day. Wait too long or take too many shallow shots at attention and you'll be left trying to talk the other into a relationship. It's never the place you want to be—begging for commitment.

"Engagement has to be heartfelt," writes Vaynerchuk, "or it won't work. . . . You cannot underestimate people's ability to spot a soulless, bureaucratic tactic a million miles away. It's a big reason why so many companies that have dipped a toe in social media waters have failed miserably."[9]

Winning friends begins with friendliness.

5
—

Access Affinity

Like. Friend. Follow. Share.

In the digital age, affinity often exists before we share the first hello. In Carnegie's time friendship and commonality walked hand in hand. You met. You talked. You found common ground and with it a fondness that led to deeper friendship. Today people follow you on Twitter or belong to the same Facebook group or "like" your latest video on YouTube before you ever meet. Often there are numerous threads of affinity before you actually meet.

With the particulars of what we like and dislike—digital buttons and thumbs-up included—we give and are given permission to make agreements and disagreements based solely on affinity. We have points of affinity and points of dissonance, and more often than not, we gravitate and grant influence to those with whom we have the most in common. This can be a tremendous boost to building lasting relationships in which influence exists.

We are not speaking of the law of attraction. You can think about having lots of friends with whom you have lots of influence, but nothing much will change if you don't take genuine, meaningful action to build those relationships. We are speaking of what author John C. Maxwell calls "the law of magnetism."

"Effective leaders are always on the lookout for good people," he writes.

> Think about it. Do you know who you're looking for right now? What is your profile of perfect employees? What qualities do these people possess? Do you want them to be aggressive and entrepreneurial? Are you looking for leaders? Do you care whether they are in their twenties, forties, or sixties? . . . Now, what will determine whether the people you want are the people you get, whether they will possess the qualities you desire? You may be surprised by the answer. Believe it or not, who you get is not determined by what you *want*. It's determined by who you *are*.[1]

Like attracts like—in character and commonality. Today, however, we can have a head start. We can ascertain affinity before we approach a person. Liking serves, in the digital age, as a perfect door to influence.

When someone joins the same Facebook group, follows your blog, or comments on a website, he or she is saying yes to you. That creates an intensely powerful position to hold if you want to influence that person.

When a person says no and really means it, a physiological cascade of reactions is taking place that is putting the person in a defensive position, ready to withdraw. But when this same person says yes and really means it, he is in a position of acceptance, of openness, of moving forward. So the more yeses you can get at the outset of an interaction, even if they have little to do with the ultimate proposal, the more likely you are to put the person in a mood to agree with you along the way.

Getting to yes is so much easier if you start with yes.

We have an obvious opportunity—a positive position from which to start dialogue. With the vast opportunities available to us to connect with the people who are interested in who we are and what we have to say, there is little excuse for starting a relationship, or even a conversation, on the wrong foot.

More than that, organizations have the power to get their constituents saying yes based purely on the influence of the community. Microsoft understood this well when it released Windows 7.

The computer giant had been dealt a blow with the exasperating launch of Windows Vista, a universally derided operating system. But it was ready to reenter the fray with Windows 7, and it had learned from past experiences. It had to get its customers, its users, onboard right from the start. It had to get them saying yes. First it had to find its fans, the potential influencers in the community of PC users.

In *Empowered*, authors Josh Bernoff and Ted Schadler explore Microsoft's strategy for getting back in the ring. To combat the slick Mac-versus-PC commercials that depicted the PC as a nerdy, inefficient, outdated number cruncher, it solicited "I'm a PC" videos directly from users via a YouTube channel. It edited them together to create a powerful beginning to their yes-based marketing campaign. When it released a beta version of Windows 7 to targeted users, it trolled the feedback on blogs, Twitter, Facebook, discussion forums, and other social communities. In preparation for the market release, it created a moderated feed of the content posted on a host of other sites and platforms and presented the feed on its website, Facebook page, and elsewhere. It created advertising featuring users, highlighting the concept that Windows 7 was designed in part as a result of customer suggestions. The tagline: "I'm a PC, and Windows 7 was my idea."

The coup de grâce, though, was how it got its fans to celebrate Windows 7 and to share it with others. It offered an opportunity to its fans—it made them feel important.

> If you were a Windows 7 fan you could sign up to have a party in your home to show off the new features—Microsoft would send along materials. . . . Word about the party opportunities spread through social media and before long, tens of thousands of people in fourteen countries had signed up. Microsoft estimates that the parties reached about eight hundred thousand people, including hosts and guests.[2]

Considering how the release of Windows Vista had gone, PC users could have said no to Windows 7 right from the start, but Microsoft got them to say yes.

When we start with yes, at the most basic level we are creating affinity. But to turn affinity into influence, there must remain a foundation of empathy. We must be able to constantly see the interaction from another's point of view so that we know the ultimate value of our points of affinity.

Rather than use social media opportunities to help us start from yes and maintain that necessary commitment, we often ignore what it is that others want and bombard them with our pitch. Instead of getting them to say, "Yes! Yes!" we force them to say, "Stop! Stop!" Social media guru Chris Brogan calls it the blizzard of business rather than a communication snowfall:

> Conversations and relationships are based on several touches. In the traditional marketing and communication world, people would use each touch to ask for something, to issue a call to action. This isn't how social networks work. . . . They are there to give you permission to reach someone who has opted into

a relationship with you. . . . It's a snowfall. Every individual flake doesn't mean a lot, but the body of work can change everything.[3]

You have to offer them what they want in your communication if you want to begin and remain at yes. Only then have you earned a level of trust that permits you to confidently offer others your pitch, whether it is for a product, service, or cause.

Of course, this principle is equally relevant and required outside of the digital realm. A newspaper company had a policy of delivering a new paper to customers who called to complain that their papers had been damaged by inclement weather. But over time rising gas prices and fewer subscriptions made it financially impossible to maintain the practice. So they sent what they believed to be a very friendly letter to their customers. It began something like this:

> *Dear valued customer,*
> *We will no longer deliver replacement newspapers when previously delivered newspapers have been damaged by weather.*

They went on to explain the change in policy. And then, at the very end of the letter, they wrote this:

> *If you do receive a damaged newspaper, please let us know and we will refund the price of the newspaper on your next bill.*

The first response customers might have when reading this letter is irritation and protest. By the end of the letter, they're too worked up to care that an alternative—and possibly a better one—is being offered.

What if, instead, the company had written the letter as follows:

> *Dear valued customer,*
>
> *We recognize how frustrating it can be when the paper you receive is damaged due to the weather.* (Yes, it is!) *You pay for a product and service and expect quality in both areas.* (Yes, I do!) *Consequently, we will now offer a full refund for any paper you receive that has been rendered unreadable because of the weather.* (Really? Great!)
>
> *We also wanted to make you aware that, like you, our business has been affected by rising gas prices. Consequently, we will no longer be able to offer to deliver replacement papers. Just call us, and you will receive a refund instead.* (Oh, okay.)

At the very least, customers might have viewed the actions of the company in a much more favorable light.

Today, there are two kinds of agreement. We need to keep both in mind where our interactions are concerned. The first kind of agreement is the common variety. It is the sort that surrounds two parties holding the same opinion on a particular issue. The presumption with this kind of agreement is that they were engaged at one time in a dialogue in which they uncovered their harmony of opinion. For most of us this sort of dialogue-based agreement is the only kind of agreement we consider.

But there is another kind of agreement that was far less feasible during Carnegie's time but has become all the more important today. This second kind of agreement is based on two parties liking the same thing—or, as we might view it, being similar people. We don't typically call this sort of harmony an "agreement," but in the digital age it is best to think of it as such because we are always drawn to those with whom we have something in common.

Establishing this commonality or affinity at the outset is a new form of yes. The more early yeses you possess, the more likely you are to succeed in capturing a yes to your idea, solution, or transaction.

Access affinity as early and often as possible.

6

Surrender the Credit

A Dale Carnegie Training student in Australia relayed the following story, which serves as a good lesson for what can happen when we ignore this principle.

My business partner and I operated one of the largest IT retailers in Brisbane. We had eight stores, employed more than sixty staff members, and had a turnover of more than $10m per year. Although my business partner had helped me a lot and he was a reasonably easygoing person, I believed all the success was contributed by me. There was only one way to run the company and it was my way. When there was a likelihood of an argument, I made sure it became an argument and tried to win it regardless of the cost. I never began our meetings in friendly fashion and often talked down to him. I never considered his feelings and even wondered why he wasn't more like me.

In the end I won all the arguments and had my way, but I lost the partnership and subsequently the company. After I learned this principle I started looking back and now understand how wrong I was. I often think if I had known these things sooner, how different my business would be today. I know I can't change the past now, but I can see the mistakes I made and try to not repeat them.

Today this gentleman is a different person. "Now I always ask my partners about their goals before I set my own," he writes. "Then I ask myself, 'What can I do to help this relationship lead to their goals?'"

While it's easy to see why we want credit for successes for which we labored, claiming the credit will never win you friends. It will also diminish your influence quicker than just about any other action.

What is the worst quality in a leader? Ask the followers and they would tell you it is the quality of taking credit when things go well and dishing out blame when things go wrong. Few postures send a clearer "It's all about me" message. Few messages send people scurrying in the other direction faster.

Who wants a friend who thinks it's all about them? Who wants a leader who doesn't see your contributions? The answers to those questions are easy.

Answering the opposite questions is just as easy: Who wants a friend who doesn't care who gets the credit? Who wants a leader who sees the full value of your contribution?

"Giving away credit is a magical multiplier," writes *Forbes* blogger August Turak, a former founding employee at MTV.

It works equally well in business and in our personal lives. But harnessing this magic requires an attitude of gratitude. Without a sincere sense of gratitude, sharing credit is just another manipulative trick bound to backfire. . . . None of this is rocket science. It's common sense. So why is credit stolen far more often than shared? The usual suspect is fear.[1]

But fear, in this case, should be reserved for the possibility of becoming a person who is afraid to share the spoils of success.

Turak shares a homily he once heard that makes this point well:

> "The Sea of Galilee is teeming with fish and life," the priest began. "The Dead Sea is dead and devoid of life. They are both fed by the sparkling water of the River Jordan, so what's the difference? The Sea of Galilee gives all its water away. The Dead Sea keeps it all for itself. Like the Dead Sea, when we keep all that is fresh and good for ourselves, we turn our lives into a briny soup of salty tears."

Surrendering the credit for a job or project can't be a false humility, a covert approach to seeking the spotlight. This is a form of the martyr syndrome. The principle suggested here is born not of attention-seeking activity but rather of a supreme confidence that you are a far better person when those around you know they play an important role not only in a collaborative success but also in your personal success.

Watch any film or music awards show and you will see this dynamic in action, especially in the more magnanimous participants. What is the first gesture expected of the winner of an award? An acceptance speech. And what are acceptance speeches but a list of thank-yous to those who were responsible for the winner's success? Some would argue this is merely standard show script, but those faces behind the names would have something else to say.

As the camera swings to show these faces, all are beaming— some even crying joyful tears, sharing in the success, and reciprocating the gratitude.

It is perhaps no coincidence that Greer Garson, the woman

credited with the longest acceptance speech in Oscar history at five and a half minutes, is also the co–record holder with Bette Davis for the most consecutive Best Actress Oscar nominations at five. Could it be that all that gratitude was a big part of the reason she was so successful?

It's often said that to be successful you must surround yourself with successful people. While there is truth to the statement, few see that there are two ways to approach this positioning. Either you can seek friendships with those who are already successful, or you can seek success for those who are already friends. Whichever way you choose, one thing is certain: your success is always commensurate with the number of people who want to see you successful. But one way provides better numbers.

When you seek friendships with those who are successful, there is no guarantee they will want success for you too. You might have to work to overcome being perceived as a relational leech. On the other hand, when you seek success for those who are already friends, you can just about guarantee that these same people will want success for you.

Surrendering the credit is a way of life you cultivate in your relationships because you are grateful for them and for what they give to you. It is nothing more than putting the success and betterment of others first—and putting your confidence in both who you are and in the rubberlike power of reciprocity.

Mark Twain certainly possessed the former; and Henry Irving could not accuse him of at least trying to put confidence in the latter. There's an amusing anecdote about a conversation between the two literary contemporaries that neatly demonstrates this principle.

Henry Irving was telling Mark Twain a story. "You haven't heard this, have you?" he inquired after the preamble. Twain assured him he had not. A little later Irving again paused and asked the same question. Twain made the same answer. Irving then got almost to the climax of the tale before breaking off again: "Are you quite sure you haven't heard this?"

The third time was too much for the listener.

"I can lie twice for courtesy's sake, but I draw the line there. I can't lie the third time at any price. I not only heard the story, I invented it."[2]

Twain would have been happy to let the awkward irony pass without a word of the actual truth. Did it really matter to him that it was his story all along? No. He was happy to have the story play well for the good of the conversation. While Twain gave in at the end—and who could blame him?—the funny story illustrates that it doesn't matter who gets the credit for a thing so long as that thing benefits all the parties involved.

Inherent in the principle of surrendering the credit to someone else is this word we've already used: "reciprocity." We don't give in order to get in a transactional sense. But we do give in order to foster relationships—and by doing so we know there will be rewards. Reciprocity is a natural by-product of a relationship where two people share in joys and pains. "Double the joy, half the sorrow," goes the saying. In true relationships friends look for ways to repay friends. What would happen if this spirit of relating spread throughout a company or a particular niche in the marketplace, or even across an entire value chain?

Two things are certain: (1) everyone involved would enjoy life a lot more, and (2) success would be more probable as collaboration occurred naturally. We have more power to spread this spirit of relating today than ever.

In the long run, no one but the originator remembers things such as whose idea it was, who spoke first, or who took the first risk. What people remember is magnanimity. It is an interesting paradox that the more you surrender the credit for something you've done, the more memorable you become, and the more you actually end up receiving credit.

President Ronald Reagan was once quoted as saying, "What I would really like to do is to go down in history as the president who made Americans believe in themselves again." From this quote alone we can establish a fairly accurate character analysis of the man. He was in the game so that others could win. His political goals centered on the uplifting and success of those he served in the office of president.

Perhaps what best typifies Reagan is the quote on the plaque that sat above his Oval Office desk. It read: "There is no limit to what a man can do, or where he can go, if he doesn't mind who gets the credit."[3]

So often this is the case for influential people. They pursue a higher calling, something that transcends whatever political, bureaucratic, or success-oriented motivations stifle others. Reagan dismissed comments about his legacy with the quip that he wouldn't be around to hear what the scholars and historians would say of him. This is what endeared him to so many as a person and leader. He lived and led with a constant surrender to the greater good of a country and did so with starkly unconventional methods. This is the mark of a person who seeks to elevate others despite himself. It is the unconventional mind that understands success isn't about attention and accolades. It's about partnerships and progress.

7

Engage with Empathy

We already discussed the debacle surrounding Armando Galarraga's almost-perfect game, destroyed by a gross umpire error on what should have been the final play. When you look at the replay you see that Galarraga's face slips from elation to disbelief in seconds. The cheers of the crowd are interrupted by an eerie silence. Then loud boos and profanity ensue.

Galarraga was needlessly robbed of what is considered the holy grail of pitching accomplishments. This is all the more maddening when you consider that the pitcher was not a superstar expected to reach such heights. He was an average journeyman who had accumulated an equal amount of wins and losses. This was perhaps his one shot at pitching prominence, and it had been spoiled. Who would blame him for lashing out at the umpire—crying out for justice? Even Joyce himself, after the game, said that if he were the pitcher, he would have been fast and fierce in the umpire's face. But there is yet another side—a third dimension—to the story.

More memorable than Galarraga's tainted perfection or Jim Joyce's subsequent contrition was the pitcher's response to the pilfering of his prize. His handling of the injustice engaged the entire world.

In an ESPN interview following the game Galarraga admitted he did not know what the call was going to be. He was just concentrating on catching the ball and getting the out. He admitted he was disappointed but conceded that the runner might have been safe. He was both nervous and excited. The intensity of the situation meant that he had to rely on the calm judgment of the umpire.

After the game, however, Galarraga viewed the replay and knew that a perfect game had just been taken from him. Yet somehow, when he spoke to the umpire he was able to say, "I know nobody is perfect." He saw Joyce's contrition and knew he had a choice: beat him down further or see things from his perspective. The consideration compelled Galarraga to offer a hug to Joyce to make him feel okay. This was no camera-ready compassion. Galarraga was sincerely disappointed *and* sincerely empathetic. Throughout the postgame interview he consistently responded to questions and the situation with the utmost nobility. He did not attempt to paint the umpire as a villain. He displayed humility and perspective, the progenitors of empathy.

In an age bent on self-promotion and interpersonal leverage, we seldom take the time to consider how someone else might feel in any given situation.

No one in the sports world would have faulted Galarraga for ripping the umpire on national television. Who would have whispered a word if the pitcher had used a featured interview as a platform to demolish Joyce's reputation?

Yet Galarraga did nothing of the sort. His comments centered on how the umpire must have felt or what he must be feeling and the acknowledgment that nobody is perfect. We marvel at this kind of reaction because it is so uncommon. Yet an intriguing and noteworthy point is that the young pitcher cemented a more memorable place in sports history for his response to losing the perfect game than he would have if he had achieved pitching perfection.

Those who can find a way to engage others in a manner worthy of such distinction are on the path of significant influence. When dealing with a person, always ask yourself, "How would I feel, how would I react, if I were in his shoes?"

"Cooperativeness in conversation," wrote Gerald S. Nirenberg, "is achieved when you show that you consider the other person's ideas and feelings as important as your own."[1]

We frequently hear critiques of the world's leaders. It is easy, as the saying goes, to sit in the stands and solve everyone else's problems. What we rarely witness are people who say, "I can't imagine the pressure you must be under to have the weight of an entire country on your shoulders. I can't imagine how much you must lie awake at night thinking through whether you made the right decision or said the right thing on national television."

Once you take the time to consider the other person's perspective, you will become sympathetic to his feelings and ideas. You will be able to authentically and honestly say, "I don't blame you for feeling as you do. If I were in your position, I would feel just as you do." This phrase, so rare in discourse today, will stop people in their tracks, will immediately get their attention, and will make them far more amenable to your ideas. Most people are merely looking for somebody who will listen to them and be sympathetic with their plight, regardless of how large or small their woes. If you can do that for another, you are giving her a gift that will brighten her day, even her week or month.

One man took a Dale Carnegie course years ago and reported how the special, genuine interest of a nurse profoundly impacted his life. Martin Ginsberg grew up poor, without a father and with a mother on welfare. One Thanksgiving day he waited alone in the hospital for orthopedic surgery. His mother had to work and couldn't be there for him; loneliness was crushing him. He pulled the covers and pillow over his head and wept.

Just then a young student nurse poked her head in, heard him sobbing, sat on his bed, pulled the covers and pillow off him, and wiped away his tears. She told him how lonely *she* was too. She had to work all day and couldn't be with her family. Then she asked young Martin whether he would have dinner with her.

He agreed.

So she went to the cafeteria and returned with two trays of Thanksgiving dinner. They talked and talked, and while she was supposed to get off work at 4:00 p.m., she stayed until 11:00 p.m., when he fell asleep.

"Many Thanksgivings have come and gone since then," Ginsberg writes, "but not one ever passes without me remembering that particular one and my feelings of frustration, fear, loneliness, and the warmth and tenderness of a stranger that somehow made it all bearable."

Today there's little excuse for misunderstanding or overlooking another's perspective. Most of us are broadcasting the details of our lives, seeking significance or a sympathetic ear from anyone who will listen. By taking time to research other people's current circumstances you will avoid making assumptions about them. If a person is important to you in some way, every second you spend trying to better understand his perspective is a second well spent.

We are not empathetic creatures naturally, so we must work at it. Many elements can factor in to how we respond in certain situations: our upbringing, our faith persuasion, our economic status, or our current career status. These and more mix with our emotions to produce a mode of personal engagement with others. Yet when we take the very things that personally move us and allow them to paint our perceptions of others, we move to a more influential place where our words can have significant impact.

We would all grow in stature and confidence if we could learn how to celebrate the most common thread in everyone. Imagine the personal barriers you could bridge in your workplace, your home, or your friendships if you could always respond to mistakes and disputes in a gracious manner. What sort of treatment would you receive back? What sort of perception would others have of you?

Remember, empathy is not a networking tactic to be learned and leveraged; it is a link to immediate affluence in human relations. It is Galarraga giving up his right to berate Jim Joyce and burning his name into the heart of every sports fan the world over. This is the undeniable power of a gracious, understanding approach.

8

Appeal to Noble Motives

We all crave transcendence—to be part of something bigger than ourselves, to be meaningful to the world and the people within it, to have it said of us that we rose above, took a stand, reached beyond, and did what was right and honorable and true. Small boys long to be the strong warrior or the heroic prince of an imaginary kingdom. Small girls long to be the clever maiden or the captivating princess at the center of a grand adventure. At a foundational level, these same desires are a reason you hold this book in your hands.

While relational improvement and business productivity are centerpieces of our lives, their importance exists because we long to be people who make a difference. Tapping this noble motive in those you'd like to influence can therefore reap great rewards. And it is likely simpler than you think.

When the British newspaper and publishing magnate Lord Northcliffe found a newspaper using a picture of him that he didn't want published, he wrote the editor a letter. He didn't say, "Please do not publish that picture of me anymore; I don't like it." He appealed to a nobler motive: the respect and love that all of us have for motherhood. He asked that the picture not be published simply because his mother did not like it.

When John D. Rockefeller Jr., wished to stop newspaper photographers from snapping pictures of his children, he too appealed to the nobler motives. He didn't say, "I don't want their pictures published." He appealed to the desire, deep in all of us, to refrain from harming children. He said: "You know how it is, boys. You've got children yourselves, some of you. And you know it's not good for youngsters to get too much publicity."

Such an approach does more than just appeal to a noble motive in another; it assigns to that person a certain nobility. It conveys the message, "You are capable of doing the right, honorable, true thing." It is a subtle compliment that essentially says, "I believe in you." These are powerful words that move people to action, as a Dale Carnegie Training graduate named Sarah learned.

She and a friend were arranging a trip to Austria and Germany for a group of ten. They contacted a coach company to arrange a transfer from Austria to Europa Park in Rust, Germany. They received a quote of 965 euros for the transfer, which they agreed to and confirmed via email. One week before the transfer, Sarah received an email from Peter, an associate in the coach company, asking her which Rust she was planning to visit with the group. Peter told Sarah that if they were visiting the Rust in Austria it would cost 965 euros, but if it was the Rust in Germany it would cost 1,889 euros.

Naturally, Sarah was angry about the sudden change in price. She knew there was little time to arrange for another transfer at a reasonable cost. She was faced with a dilemma. Should she begin sending an angry litany of emails to Peter regarding how he changed his offer? Or was there another way to handle the problem?

Sarah determined that berating Peter would accomplish little and would still leave her stuck with the transfer problem. So she decided on a different approach. She would appeal to Peter's noble motives and attempt to fix the problem through honest interaction.

She acted calmly. She replied to his email by asking him if there were two different Europa Parks in two different cities called Rust. Peter replied in the negative.

Sarah replied with another email, including a copy of his initial offer, and explained that she had clearly specified that the transfer was for Europa Park, Rust, Germany, and that, based on his reply, there was only one. She then concluded, "I kindly request an explanation for this change of pricing, as I am sure as a respectful company, you value your initial offers, and care about maintaining your credibility with your clients."

Sarah received an apology from Peter the next day, explaining that there had been some confusion on their end. He then gladly confirmed the initial offer.

By appealing to Peter's and his company's nobler motives, Sarah was able to solve the problem without further financial or emotional cost.

Most of us do not recognize these noble desires in ourselves while we are children, but when we grow up we see them in our children and feel them well up inside of us when we watch films such as *The King's Speech, Gladiator,* or *Little Women.* In some way we all want our everydayness to include heroic elements.

"What if?" writes author and former marriage and family counselor John Eldredge, "What if those deep desires in our hearts are telling us the truth, revealing to us the life that we were *meant* to live."[1] Few would refute that there is something noble and redeemable in everyone.

All of us, being idealists at heart and preferring to present ourselves in the best light, like to think of motives that sound good. If we provide an opportunity for others to do the same, if we don't assume that their motives are selfish or deceitful, we allow them to increase their own self-worth in their response to us. We allow them to prove us right about them.

Today's advertisers are exceptionally good at applying this principle. Consider the campaigns for environmentally friendly products, Dove's Campaign for Real Beauty, and other products that make either the buyer or the company seem nobler in motive. Nonprofit organizations also employ this tactic and use social media to propagate their messages in these ways. This works because most people will react favorably to your proposals if they feel that you admire them for being honest, unselfish, and fair.

One morning at breakfast, University of San Francisco business professor David Batstone learned that one of his favorite restaurants in the Bay Area was using slave labor. The newspaper article that exposed the atrocity detailed how the restaurant forced employees to work under harsh conditions by threatening to expose their status as illegal immigrants.

The story caught David off-guard and ignited a passion within him to start the Not for Sale Campaign, an organization that seeks, among other things, to expose modern-day slave labor in communities and companies across America.

To hear David speak about the campaign is to be compelled to join in. This is precisely what he wants to see happen. He knows the issue will touch everyone. The thought of slave labor in this day and age is appalling—it makes us indignant and ready to rise up to help.

In 2010 David and his team rolled out a new initiative called Free2Work. The program is actually an app for your smartphone. The consumer scans a product, and the app then produces a grade for the company that makes the product. If, for example, you want to buy a shirt from Patagonia, you can scan the item and the Free2Work app will give Patagonia a manufacturing grade indicating how well the company performs with regard to fair trade, employment, and overseas manufacturing.

The app provides a new level of accountability for manufacturing companies and a new level of responsibility for consumers. We can't claim ignorance anymore for supporting companies that employ slave labor or fail to be transparent in their international manufacturing efforts.

On a deeper level, the app speaks directly to the noble motives of the companies involved. When held accountable for their business dealings and asked to meet a high and humane standard, companies tend to comply. They understand that consumers increasingly care about how products are made and how their companies treat the people they employ.

The Free2Work Campaign targets the noble motives of consumers and manufacturing companies to incite positive cultural change. How can you begin targeting the noble desires of your constituents and vendors in a way that will contribute to changing the ethos of a particular industry that may need new life, new standards?

This is an important question to answer today. The key to successful growth and positive impact inside and outside the marketplace is what digital maven Amy Martin calls "the business of humanity." Her response to the 2011 tsunami in Japan exemplifies the power of appealing to noble motives in the digital age.[2] It also serves as a candid reminder of the consequences of not embodying this principle.

During a late-night workout on an elliptical machine, Martin was perusing others' Twitter updates on her iPad. The earthquake and subsequent tsunami hit in Japan, and suddenly the Twittersphere was inundated with the news. She flipped to CNN on the television and caught live footage of vehicles being washed away and people frantically trying to outrun the crushing tide coming ashore. "I wasn't sure what to do," she blogged, "but I felt accountable and compelled to help in some way."

She began sifting through the most relevant tweets and links and redistributing them to her large following. She also asked her followers to send her any valuable information they had that she could broadcast to others. For four hours she continued, and none of it had anything to do with marketing or promoting products. It was about "people coming together through a virtual medium to help each other," she wrote. "It was the business of humanity."

Still, during her humanitarian efforts she witnessed an alarming contrast—large television news outlets seemingly crippled by an ill-timed concern for ratings. While she was in the midst of the digital effort, certain prominent news channels toggled back and forth between dramatic footage of the catastrophe and the latest celebrity spectacle.

"I was aghast," she wrote. "In my opinion, if these news organizations are in the least concerned about the way the public perceives their brand then they should exercise more discernment and care more about saving lives than the Hollywood beat. . . . Sometimes you need to put [Hollywood] in the backseat and focus on the right thing to do."

Martin clarifies something that is easy to forget amid the push to transactional effect. The many social media channels to which we are privy are first and foremost interpersonal communication tools designed for humans to connect. "They weren't invented," she notes, "for marketers."

Many of Martin's followers echoed the sentiment in her blog post and appreciated her appeal to the noble motives not only in the large news organizations but also in all who had the capacity to help those suffering in the wake of the tsunami. While Martin was selling nothing that night, it is no wonder 1.3 million people follow her on Twitter and some of the most prominent businesses, celebrities, and professional sports teams call on her for digital guidance. She is one who knows that doing business in the digital age is predicated on doing the business of humanity well.

So often we are content to simply plug others into our digital world and browse them like commodities until we are ready to engage in some sort of transaction. Such sentiment removes the nobility inherent in our shared humanity. It makes our relationships merely tools of transaction rather than transcendence.

To truly connect with people you must celebrate their inherent dignity. In doing so you celebrate yours. Appeal to noble motives and you can move the masses, and yourself along with them.

9
—

Share Your Journey

Peddling ice to Inuits? Selling seawater to a dolphin? Compelling consumers to wear cotton? Today the last of those doesn't seem like a stretch. Examine the threads of every clothing item you own and chances are high many if not most of them are cotton. But in the 1970s that was probably not the case. Polyester and its synthetic cousins were the rage. They didn't wrinkle, they resisted stains, and they were formfitting—and as a result, cotton's market share dwindled to about 33 percent.[1]

The industry decided to fight back. It needed to make cotton desirable again, so it did what any industry would do: it started a trade association, hired ad firms, and rebranded cotton.

The slogan they settled on to save their industry? "Cotton: The fabric of our lives."

They had celebrities pitch the slogan. Barbara Walters famously donned a Hawaiian shirt, looked into the camera, and said, "Cotton . . . it's making my life comfortable today."[2]

When the cotton industry was on the line, its members made the strategic decision that the best way to get people to buy their threads was by threading cotton into a personal story. Cotton wasn't a soft, white, fluffy fiber that was spun into threads that became fabric that became garments; cotton gave life meaning by tying it together into a beautiful story. Today cotton commands about two-thirds of the market.[3]

People don't want to be treated as commodities, but more than that, they don't want to see their lives as ordinary. People want to know that they matter, and the best way to show them that they do is by allowing them to connect with a larger story. People and businesses that understand this principle are unbeatable.

In 2011, Apple topped *Fortune's* survey of business people as the world's most admired company for the fourth year in a row.[4] Part of the company's secret is found in one of the most famous TV ads in history.

In 1984, during the Super Bowl, Apple unveiled its Macintosh personal computer for the first time. The ad was aimed at distinguishing the radically new and creativity-encouraging Mac from the conformity of the masses (to Apple, that was IBM).

In the ad an athletic young woman carrying a large hammer runs into a room of look-alike, dress-alike pseudo-people. She throws the hammer at a great screen and destroys an Orwellian Big Brother–type figure. It is the dawning of a new day. Treating people as mere Social Security numbers with arms and legs is over. One-on-one business was the wave of the future.

The proof of this concept isn't found just in Apple's success; it is also found in some simple shoes.

Blake Mycoskie started TOMS shoes after a story disrupted his life. He was traveling in the developing world when he noticed a simple problem: the kids he saw had no shoes. No shoes meant a lot of other nos in their stories . . . a lot of deprivation. So Blake decided to start a company that would match every pair of shoes purchased with a pair of new shoes for a child in need.

The first year he had the pleasure of giving away ten thousand shoes. Today that number is over one million. But that's not where the story ends. One afternoon in an airport waiting area Mycoskie noticed a girl wearing a red pair of his shoes. Without revealing his identity, he asked about them. The girl told him the whole story behind TOMS in such detail that it rivaled his own description of the company. It was a moment that made him realize, "The truth is, what's inside this box is not nearly as important as what it represents. TOMS is no longer a shoe company; it's a one-for-one company."

"In addition to attracting the interest of mainstream media starting with *Vogue, Time* and *People* magazine, TOMS Shoes attracted prestigious partners," explains power blogger Valeria Maltoni. "Ralph Lauren, who had not partnered with anyone for 40 years, joined in with TOMS Shoes for the rugby brand. The ad agency working with AT&T created a commercial to tell the 'authentic story' of how Blake used their network to stay in touch and work on the go."

Maltoni concludes her thoughts on the success of TOMS with an insightful nod to the power of this principle: "People remember. And when a message is a mission, they will tell your story to anyone who will hear it—even a stranger at an airport. And by doing that, they become your strongest advocates in marketing your product. . . . The lesson: influence is given."[5]

While larger stories can be inviting, the land of small, personal stories can be intimidating. It is one thing to reveal a cause, cure, or commodity. It is another thing entirely to reveal yourself.

In April 2003, author David Kuo was driving home from a party with his wife. He woke up in the ER, told he had a brain tumor likely to kill him in a matter of months.

At three o'clock on that Palm Sunday morning, David and his wife, Kim, faced a decision: How much of their story did they want people to know? How willing were they to share it?

The tendency was to remain private. But they resisted that impulse, and Kim started calling friends, telling them the story and telling them to tell others so that they could pray. Within hours a page for them was set up on CaringBridge.org, a nonprofit site where people facing serious illness can post updates, needs, and anything else that they would like.

In the weeks and months that followed, the Kuos decided that the more information they could share, the more people they could help—they knew they were hardly alone in their cancer battle. That decision was life-changing for them. They saw their story as part of something far larger than them. It eventually provided a type of opportunity for them with other people facing similar challenges.

Their first bit of advice for everyone? Share your story.

That's something Ann M. Baker from Seattle, Washington, learned in a Dale Carnegie Training course:

> Most people treasure their privacy, as I do. However, when faced with breast cancer, chemotherapy, and radiation treatments, I did not want to share the worry and the pain.
> But when my cancer news slipped out among family, friends, and coworkers, I was overwhelmed with email encouragement. Even family acquaintances whom I had never met emailed their breast cancer stories, including phone numbers and follow-on get-well cards.
> This amazing outpouring of courage and love started a recovery journey that has changed my life. . . . And thanks to email, I know that no one needs or wants to journey the cancer road alone. For life is not about me. It is about us.

There's nothing wrong if something that is "about us" is also "good for me." One digital media blogger with more than a million followers put out the word that she was going to have Lasik surgery to correct her eyesight. Not only was she going to have the surgery, she was going to stream it live on her blog for all who were interested in having the surgery themselves. Transparency became her currency. She not only got 20/15 vision, she got better insight into a whole new way of using the digital world to share our personal journeys with others. She cites the live stream of a friend's recent wedding or a client's use of live streaming video to watch his son's football games when he's away on business as good examples.

"Aside from sports, entertainment and marketing, what else can live video be used for?" she asks. "Will it be adopted as a new communication channel used for functional benefit? . . . What about weddings, graduations, club meetings, religious ceremonies, birthdays, coaching, instructional content, cooking classes, births or even funerals? The opportunities are endless if they are embraced."[6]

People trudge through most days with little excitement in their lives. But our digital age provides so many opportunities to give people an authentic view of who you are or what your company strives to be, thus creating touch points of commonality that draw you into closer friendship with others. It is easy to make a video instead of presenting a few drawings. It is easy to create a dynamic website to support a new company or organization. It is easy to use video conferencing instead of a call and to show a compelling presentation to all involved instead of simply telling them. But people have come to expect these things, too.

To really make your idea pop, take a unique approach. Step beyond the bounds of your computer and do something people don't see every day. Use all of the tools available to you and your imagination to make your ideas vivid, interesting, and dramatic.

Share your stories, and others will be willing to share theirs. Together you will create a new and larger story.

More and more common—and commonly effective at building influential relationships—is the authentic intersection of personal and professional life. While this intersection will always have certain judicious boundaries, many of the historically businesslike boundaries have been lowered or removed altogether today because most people have come to remember that the short- and long-term success of all interactions—transactional or otherwise—rides on the depth of the relationship. The more a colleague, friend, or customer shares of your journey, the more you can accomplish together.

When your journey is our journey, we are both compelled to see where it goes.

10

Throw Down a Challenge

When it comes to discussions about the best players in NBA history, two names usually come up: Larry and Magic.

Larry Bird and Earvin "Magic" Johnson were, individually, two of the most compelling players to ever grace the hardwood courts—gifted passers who possessed almost otherworldly senses of players and positions on the basketball court. They were virtually unrivaled in clutch situations. They prided themselves for their defense as much as for their offense, and they worked harder than any of their teammates.

And they defined basketball for a decade. Magic beat Larry in the 1979 NCAA championship, then beat him again in the 1984 NBA Championship. Larry beat Magic in 1985 and then lost to him again in 1987.

For most of their careers they didn't much like each other, but their respect for each other knew no bounds. Then in 1991, Magic was unexpectedly forced to retire from professional basketball because he contracted HIV. The day after Magic's announcement, Bird found himself preparing for a regular-season game. He stretched his back, loosened up by jogging through the corridors of the arena, shot baskets from his usual spots on the floor . . . and for the first time in his life he had no desire to play. His competitor, who by then had become his friend, was gone from the sport. Magic had played a major role in making Bird who he was.

A few months later, at his retirement ceremony, Magic said, "I want to thank Larry Bird personally for bringing out the best in Magic Johnson because, without you, I could have never risen to the top."[1]

Some people seem to think that competition is a dirty word. It isn't. Competition is one of the most compelling realities of the natural world. While connection is necessary to keep us thriving, competition is necessary to keep us striving.

"As iron sharpens iron," wrote King Solomon, Israel's third monarch, "so one man sharpens another."[2]

The sound of iron sharpening iron is about as subtle as the sound of fingernails on a chalkboard. But King Solomon recognized that the only way to get the best out of yourself and others is to challenge and collide. While a life of permanent interpersonal pleasantries appears more comfortable and sounds more peaceful, a relationally complacent life is a fruitless life.

A challenge doesn't have to involve blood, sweat, and tears. Coke issued a challenge to consumers in a 2010 social media ad campaign—they challenged people not to smile.

Coke set up a special vending machine on a real college campus. This machine didn't just dispense soft drinks. It surprised students with everything from free bottles of Coke to a bouquet of flowers, a pizza, and a six-foot sub.[3]

The cameras caught it all, and the results were streamed to YouTube. The sheer joy and surprise of the students receiving the gifts—some high-fiving, others hugging, all smiling and laughing—also put smiles on the faces of the nearly four million viewers who watched it online. The challenge to viewers was not to smile, and it garnered millions of willing failures, just as Coke had hoped for.

One of the things that drove the early, wild days of the Internet was the passionate competition between Microsoft and AOL. Easily forgotten in this era of Apple and Google, the AOL/Microsoft battle accelerated the availability of cutting-edge services for the customer. Each company envisioned the day when consumers would perform the majority of their transactions online, get most of their information online, and live a big chunk of their lives online.

The companies loathed each other, and their cultures were vastly different—one was a consumer-oriented marketing company that happened to use technology and the other was a technology company that happened to use consumer marketing.[4] AOL testified against Microsoft in the antitrust trial against the giant software company. And yet that competition made both companies larger and more successful than either would have been without the other.

Yes, everyone faces challenges in their lives, and people commonly say it doesn't matter what the challenge is; what matters is how one responds to it.

True enough.

Some people get injured or sick or hurt and give up. They put themselves on the conveyor belt to the grave.

Others rise to great heights. Take Teddy Roosevelt, for example. A sickly child, young Teddy had life-threatening asthma. Oftentimes he struggled to breathe, and the asthma weakened his heart. Then, when he was twelve, his father put down a challenge: "Theodore, you have the mind but you have not the body, and without the help of the body the mind cannot go as far as it should. You must make your body. It's hard drudgery to make one's body, but I know you will do it."[5]

In response, the boy half grinned and half snarled—the first reported instance of the look that would become known the world over. He then jerked his head back and replied through clenched teeth, "I'll make my body."[6]

Over the next year his life consisted of strenuous exercise. And as his strength grew, so did his boldness and daring. He plunged into icy rivers and climbed seven mountains, including one of them twice in a single day. And as he did these things his obsession with nature began. Everything from birds to moss fascinated him, and he collected several hundred specimens for preservation in the "Roosevelt Museum of Natural History."[7]

Without his father's challenge, what might have become of such a sickly boy? The challenge changed him forever.

It is also true, however, that the challenge itself is just as important as the response to it. Challenges that inspire and compel are very different from challenges that discourage and depress.

In 2010, Shaun King, pastor of Courageous Church in Atlanta, wanted to raise money for a permanent home for disabled Haitian orphans. But how to do it? This was the first challenge. In the digital age, creativity in such matters is greatly expanded. He wanted to reach the biggest audience possible with the message. He came up with the idea for a celebrity charity auction with a twist. People wouldn't be bidding for a picture, an autograph, or a date. They'd bid for a celebrity to follow them on Twitter and retweet their posts. He approached *Desperate Housewives* star Eva Longoria Parker with the challenge. She jumped in and then challenged her celebrity buddies to become part of it as well. They did, and TwitChange was born.[8]

In 2010, more than 175 celebrities with a combined ninety million followers garnered thirty million hits and raised more than $500,000.[9] That's the power of a meaningful challenge in an age where our reach is long and influence expansive.

There are pernicious half-truths in the world, but few are as disturbing as "Go along to get along." That isn't a way to live a life, raise a family, or run a business. People don't want to be leveled down; they want to be leveled up. They want their vision raised, and sometimes that means throwing down a challenge.

Charles Schwab once said, "The way to get things done is to stimulate competition." When we compete, we are striving to win because winning generates a feeling of success and importance. When victory is defined as team victory—for a cause, a country, a cure, or a company—winning is all the more compelling, because the competition forces us to communicate and connect on an area of affinity. The competition comes to mean as much to us for its camaraderie as for its ultimate result.

Look around your sphere of influence for an area of affinity that can generate a competition that can mean something more than reaching the finish line—something that can mean lasting friendships and corporate influence for positive change. If it's one person you'd like to help change, throw down a compelling challenge that gets you both involved in the arena. Nobody said challenges were clean endeavors. Get dirty for the sake of others, and they will get dirty for you.

Part 4

How to Lead Change Without Resistance or Resentment

1

Begin on a Positive Note

In his classic book *Leadership Is an Art,* author Max DePree famously asserted, "The first responsibility of a leader is to define reality. The last is to say thank you. In between, the leader is a servant."[1] A tendency is to take the assertion to mean we must bear down and get the ugly stuff said first, as though it were to the leader's advantage to get the bad news out of the way. But this is not the case, especially in a day and age when bad news travels at the speed of light.

While a current relationship, whether between a company and its customers or between two individuals, might be strained or even in serious trouble, it does little good to start off a conversation on a negative note. Like a play whose first act features a tragedy, it sets a gloomy and unpleasant stage. Shoulders sag, faces fall, and hearts begin to sink inside the recipients. Imagine this effect spread viruslike throughout the ranks of an organization or across a company's entire value chain or across an entire country. You will be forced to work against a wave of negative psychological and physiological reactions from the start, and even if you can overcome them quickly, there's no need to spend the little time you may have trying to undo something that could have been avoided in the first place.

Instead, begin a conversation with honest and genuine appreciation; the receiver will be more amenable to your ideas and less defensive or resistant.

Many of us have experienced that defensiveness and resistance when dealing with customer service agents—amazingly enough! But Sanjiv Ekbote, who had recently read *How to Win Friends and Influence People,* knew how to handle a difficult situation.[2]

He had recently purchased a house with a home warranty. One evening the bathroom faucet began to leak, so he called the warranty company. And within four hours, a young technician arrived to fix the problem. First he replaced the valve, but the water began flowing faster. So the technician capped the pipe, but the water pressure broke seals and water began leaking inside the walls.

Sanjiv was upset and immediately called the warranty company to ask them to send a more experienced technician. He could have ranted and raved at the person who answered the phone, but instead he paused. He calmly provided his information, and then he thanked the representative for sending out a technician so quickly. He explained what had happened, and the woman tracked down an expert technician, scheduled the earliest appointment possible, and waived the service fee.

If Sanjiv had reacted differently, would he have received the same service?

This seems like a rather simple technique, yet it is deceptively difficult to practice. Let's consider DePree's mandate for leaders to understand why. At the heart of our misinterpretation of his statement is the connotation that the term "reality" carries in our daily discourse. Why is it that we have to "face reality," deliver "a dose of reality" that is reluctantly swallowed like foul medicine, bring someone "back to reality" from an idyllic dreamland that doesn't jibe with the hard-nosed facts? This is the mind-set from which we often approach crucial conversations.

Is reality actually a bitter pill, or at least an overly pragmatic one? Probably not, but we may be hardwired to see it that way, particularly when something is nagging at us. Our hunter-gatherer ancestry still dictates that we pay particular attention to the most dramatic unfolding around us, and usually these are negative ones. Our survival depends on this ability—or it once did, anyway. Neuroscientists, in a variety of studies, have shown that "we care more about the threat of bad things than we do about the prospect of good things. Our negative brain tripwires are far more sensitive than our positive triggers," wrote Ray Williams, a leadership coach.[3] We even remember negative events better, or at least our memories are skewed toward them.

Unfortunately, research has shown that this effect isn't limited to events but extends to the impressions we form of other people. We may weigh those traits or behaviors we deem to be negative more heavily than the positive, particularly if they are moral or ethical in nature.[4]

At those times when we hope most strongly to encourage change in others, we are often frustrated with current conduct. Our brains are preoccupied with the negative behavior. It shapes our perception of reality. It crowds out the positive. And so it is no surprise that in our communications we can't seem to help jumping into the problem—or, from our listeners' perspectives, the criticism.

Our listeners' brains are just like ours. The negative or critical in what we say becomes their point of obsession. It drowns out all possibility of discovering the positive opportunities within the conversation. I'm sure you've seen it happen: faces grow tight, expressions become studiously blank, and only the eyes may reveal the inner rant of protest that is blocking out anything else you might have to say.

If we don't work hard to avoid this drama, we shoot ourselves in the leadership foot. In a classic study on how negative and positive feedback affect performance, J. Sidney Shrauger and Saul Rosenberg discovered, quite simply, that our performance suffers when we receive feedback that we have failed in some way.[5] Now, if we are confident and have strong self-esteem, the effect is less severe. However, a secondary reaction to criticism is to discount the validity of the feedback—we reject it outright, so it has little effect on our behavior except to sully our attitude.

Why take the risk? Why not mitigate these effects on performance or attitude right from the start?

In an article on leadership skills for teachers, Trent Lorcher explained how, as a basketball coach, he had handled a disappointing loss with his team. "We lost an important game on account of several missed free throws. My natural reaction was to yell at my team. Instead, I praised them for being aggressive and getting to the free throw line consistently. We then practiced free throws for the next hour. My players, already upset by the loss, responded well to praise."[6]

In his latest book, *Good Boss, Bad Boss,* Robert Sutton, an organizational psychologist, relates a story sent to him by a former U.S. Army officer. Most of the man's superior officers were jerks—nasty, belittling, and mean-spirited. But his battalion commander was different.

> I got out of a line a few times and he brought me in immediately and counseled me on my behavior. He didn't yell or belittle me, but I got the point and was embarrassed that I had let him down. I'm a better person for it and I'd like to think that I have picked up his habits and that I emulate his actions by treating people the way they should be treated.[7]

We can overcome our baser instincts by acknowledging our inherent tendencies and working to focus our attention on the positive. It's not just positive thinking; it's rewiring our brains to recognize that our perceptions are not necessarily in line with truth, stopping to analyze our underlying assumptions about a situation, and questioning those assumptions until we get to a fuller picture. We can train our mirror-neuron systems—those cells discovered in recent decades that enable us to understand the actions of others, to interpret their intentions, and to predict what they might do next—to include positive behaviors and what they reveal about the people we coach.

And that is essential if we want to be authentic in our appreciation. We need to find a truthful positive point to begin from, and we need to show appreciation that resonates with the receiver. The best bosses, according to Robert Sutton, take the time to discover how each member of their teams think and act. It isn't easy. Leaders, despite their best efforts, are often naturally removed from situations that may be the most revealing about individual personal dynamics. But making the effort is worth the payout in terms of influence and effectiveness as a leader.

When we acknowledge the value a person has to our organization, we establish a positive tone for open communication.

Of course, we must get around to the matter at hand eventually. Perhaps worse than attempting to get the bad news out of the way is attempting to soften it or simply not address it at all. This "Mum Effect"—a term coined by psychologists Sidney Rosen and Abraham Tesser in the early 1970s—happens because people want to avoid becoming the target of others' negative emotions.[8] We all have the opportunity to lead change, yet it often requires of us the courage to deliver bad news to our superiors. We don't want to be the innocent messenger who falls before a firing line. When our survival instincts kick in, they can override our courage until the truth of a situation gets watered down into pabulum. "The Mum Effect and the resulting filtering can have devastating effects in a steep hierarchy," writes Sutton.

"What starts out as bad news becomes happier and happier as it travels up the ranks—because after each boss hears the news from his or her subordinates, he or she makes it sound a bit less bad before passing it up the chain."[9]

Leading with the positive and resisting the urge to promote drama are tools that can help us bolster our resolve, techniques for stepping confidently into the breach. And leaders who model this behavior are less likely to be blindsided by catastrophes they should have known about all along.

At Sonda, Andrés Navarro found a way to institutionalize this approach by adopting a three-for-one rule. "We try to criticize as little as we can. We have a rule. If you get into this company and you find someone whom you don't like and you think doesn't do his work the way he should, don't say anything. Write it down on a piece of paper." People are then required to discover at least three good things about the person before they can open a discussion designed to change the other's behavior.[10]

How, then, do we engage in interactions in which undesirable topics must be discussed? We know intuitively it is always easier to listen to unpleasant things after we have heard some praise of our good points. If the praise is contrived or if the segue from praise to criticism is too abrupt, then this principle will fail. To avoid this, consider the following.

First, the praise you offer must be genuine and heartfelt, not just a tool to bide time while you compose your criticisms.

Second, you must be able to create a smooth flow from point to point.

Third, offer constructive advice rather than criticism following the praise.

This style of communicating a point can be particularly difficult in written form. Without the natural flow of a conversation that presents opportunities to segue from one topic to the next, it may seem to the other person that you were just "buttering her up." If the topic is particularly contentious, you should really have a face-to-face conversation.

Many people begin their criticism with sincere praise followed by the word "but," which signals that the criticism is about to begin. This may make the listener question the sincerity of the praise. Use "and" instead, and provide constructive advice rather than criticism. This is possibly the most effective way to address an issue in written form without seeming false in your praise.

Beginning with praise and appreciation will help you help employees be more productive, vendors be more committed, and friends and family be more inclined to see your point of view. A positive outlook always places interactions on a positive path.

2

Acknowledge Your Baggage

Beth was a high-level executive in a Fortune 100 company. While much loved by her bosses and her team, she was in the throes of battle with a colleague, Harvey, who headed up another division. All's fair in love and war, right? Well, Beth was living by that motto, revealing her most vindictive side in their interactions.

But Beth wanted to be a better leader, and so she enlisted the aid of Marshall Goldsmith, executive coach and author of *What Got You Here Won't Get You There*. What she learned is that while she was respected by many, her behavior with Harvey was still affecting her reputation. She needed to negotiate a peace agreement with Harvey, and to do so, she had to admit fault.

This might be one of the hardest situations in which to follow this approach—one in which you have to acknowledge your mistakes to the person those mistakes have harmed. Tensions on both sides are already high, competition may be a driving factor, and you may feel it isn't safe to make yourself vulnerable. Yet these are also the situations that can be most effectively defused by talking about your own mistakes first.

So what did Beth say?

"You know, Harvey, I've got a lot of feedback here, and the first thing I want to say is that I'm positive about a lot of it. The next thing I want to say is that there are some things at which I want to be better. I've been disrespectful to you, the company, and the traditions in the company. Please accept my apologies. There is no excuse for this behavior."[1]

Harvey's response? He got tears in his eyes, admitted that he too had behaved dishonorably, and declared that together they would improve.

A lengthy, embittered turf war ended simply by proclaiming the mistakes she had made.

It isn't nearly so difficult to be open to a conversation that may include a discussion of your faults if the other person begins by humbly admitting that she too is far from impeccable. Admitting one's mistakes—even when one hasn't corrected them—can help convince somebody to change his behavior.

Carnegie, the ever-effective communicator, applied this same lesson when writing on it. He began the discussion with a story of how he had failed as a mentor and coach to help readers become open to the idea. It's a subtle and masterly strategy—and proof that it can be effective in many forms.

The difficulty that leaders face in implementing this strategy rests on one critical element: you must admit that you have made mistakes, that you are fallible. Leaders across the globe struggle with this, even though most understand inherently the value of it. And if they don't understand it inherently, research certainly supports it.

Researchers at the Institute for Health and Human Potential conducted a study of thirty-five thousand people on the factors in career advancement. The item found to be most linked to career advancement? Freely admitting to making mistakes.[2]

Admitting you have made a mistake is like the first step in a twelve-step program: it is both the hardest and the most important. Until we accept accountability, how can we learn from our mistakes, use them to propel us forward, and encourage others to trust us? "To leave the road of continual failure, a person must first utter the three most difficult words to say: 'I was wrong.' He has to open his eyes, admit his mistakes, and accept complete responsibility for his current wrong actions and attitudes."[3]

Portia Nelson poetically describes this process in her "Autobiography in Five Short Chapters." What begins in many of our first chapters as a pit of despair progresses only to detachment from the problem until we are able to accept responsibility for our faults. Once we see the link between where we are and what we do, only then do we begin to see quicker solutions to our problems; only then do we begin to walk around the deep holes in our path altogether. Eventually we learn we can simply walk down a less problematic path. That is to say, we move from merely being proficient problem solvers to behaving more proficiently.[4]

Aside from the personal gains of admitting our mistakes, the trust it builds with our colleagues and customers, our friends and families, and our community members is invaluable. Marshall Goldsmith writes, "No one expects us to be right all the time. But when we're wrong, they certainly expect us to own up to it. In that sense, being wrong is an opportunity—an opportunity to show what kind of person and leader we are. . . . How well you own up to your mistakes makes a bigger impression than how you revel in your successes."[5]

When we talk about our mistakes, it makes us human. It becomes easier for people to relate to us. They feel we understand their perspective better. And in this mental space, they are more open to our advice.

What is lovely about this principle is that we all make mistakes and so have an ample supply of stories to use when trying to put someone at ease. Remember to follow the story with constructive advice, not straight-up criticism.

How did Carnegie use the principle with his niece and new assistant, Josephine? By considering her lack of experience and his own blunders at her age and experience level.

"You have made a mistake, Josephine," he would begin, "but Lord knows, it's no worse than many I have made. Judgment comes only with experience, and you are better than I was at your age. I have been guilty of so many silly things myself I have very little inclination to criticize you or anyone. But don't you think it would have been wiser if you had done so-and-so?"

By admitting your own mistakes, you direct the other person's attention away from his own; you soften the approach and avoid raising his defenses immediately.

When you acknowledge your baggage, trust builds naturally.

3

Call Out Mistakes Quietly

During the first days of his presidency, Coolidge and his family had not yet left their third-floor suite at the Willard Hotel in Washington. In the early morning hours the president awoke to see a cat burglar going through his clothes, removing a wallet and a watch chain. Coolidge spoke: "I wish you wouldn't take that. . . . I don't mean the watch and chain, only the charm. Read what is engraved on the back of it."

The burglar read: "Presented to Calvin Coolidge, Speaker of the House, by the Massachusetts General Court."

Coolidge then identified himself as the president, persuaded the burglar to relinquish the watch charm, led him into a quiet conversation, found out that the young man and his college roommate were unable to pay their hotel bill and buy train tickets back to their campus, counted out $32 from the wallet (which the dazed young man had also relinquished), declared it to be a loan, and advised the student that in order to avoid the Secret Service, he should leave as unconventionally as he had entered.[1]

Calling attention indirectly to someone's mistakes or missteps works wonders with people who may resent any direct criticism—and that defines most people.

Leaders of all kinds have a fantastic tool available to them for sending a subtle message about the behavior they are trying to encourage. They simply have to model that behavior themselves. And if they do not, the message to those around them will be loud and clear: "I tell you I want you to behave in such a way, but it's not actually that important. Otherwise, I would do it myself."

This concept is John Maxwell's thirteenth law of leadership in his classic *The 21 Irrefutable Laws of Leadership*. He calls it "The Law of the Picture" because people do what they see. He tells the story of platoon leader Dick Winters of Easy Company during World War II. Winters believed that it was an officer's responsibility to go first, set an example, lead the charge, and take risks alongside his men.

> One of the most remarkable incidents demonstrating Winters's way of leading by example occurred soon after D-Day on the road to Carentan, a town that Easy Company need to take from the Germans. As the American paratroopers under his command approached the town, they became pinned down by German machine-gun fire. Huddled in ditches on either side of the road, they wouldn't move forward when ordered to. Yet if they didn't move, they would eventually be cut to pieces. Winters tried rallying them. He coaxed them. He kicked them. He ran from one ditch to the other as machine-gun bullets flew by. Finally, he jumped into the middle of the road, bullets glancing off the ground near him, and shouted at the men to get moving. Everyone got up and moved forward as one. And they helped to take the town.[2]

At times it isn't possible to influence others by modeling behavior, either because you aren't with the people you are trying to influence or because you actually aren't immersed in what it is that they are doing. How do we influence behavior then? The authors of *Influencer* offer some compelling advice for these situations:

- Identify those in the group, team, family, or community who have the most influence over others and get them to model the behavior you want to promote.
- Develop a community approach to the behavior by appealing to the broader good. Peer pressure goes a long way toward influencing the thoughts and actions of individuals.
- Make any changes possible to the resources available or the environment to make the new behavior or mind-set easy to adopt.[3]

At the end of World War II, soldiers were returning from the front lines and reentering the workforce. In the process, they were displacing the women who had stepped up and filled many positions in their absence. Many women chose to remain in the workforce, which created animosity between the sexes in the workplace but also gave rise to a new view of the role women could play in the American economy.

Restaurants around the country were facing a particular struggle. The returning soldiers were granted positions as cooks. The women who had held those positions were demoted to waitresses, positions of lower pay. The result: an antagonistic relationship between cooks and waitresses in an environment in which cooperation is a necessity. Everybody suffered, including the patrons, who often received late or wrong orders. Employees were quitting and restaurants were losing customers.

So the National Restaurant Association enlisted the help of William Foote Whyte, a professor at the University of Chicago, to solve the problem. He observed the activity in a sample of restaurants, watching as cooks and waitresses slung insults, ignored each other, and behaved vindictively (at the expense of the customer).

"While many consultants might have been tempted to alter this unhealthy social climate by teaching interpersonal skills, conducting team-building exercises, or changing the pay system, Whyte took a different approach," explained the authors. "In his view, the best way to solve the problem was to change the way employees communicated."[4]

Working with a pilot restaurant, Whyte recommended they use a simple metal spindle to place orders with the kitchen. The waitresses would put the orders on the spindle and the cooks would fulfill the orders in whatever way was most efficient, but making sure that those that were placed first were prioritized.

The results were immediate: decreased conflict, decreased customer complaints, and communication and behavior that were more respectful on both sides.

Sometimes the best way to correct behavior is not to openly punish the wrong behavior but to use the situation as a platform for building self-confidence and deeper connection. Bob Hoover, a famous test pilot and frequent performer at air shows, was flying back to his home in Los Angeles from an air show in San Diego. At three hundred feet in the air, both engines suddenly stopped. By deft maneuvering he managed to land the plane and save himself and two others on board. But it was badly damaged.

Hoover's first act after the emergency landing was to inspect the airplane's fuel. Just as he suspected, the World War II propeller plane had been fueled with jet fuel rather than gasoline. Upon returning to the airport, he asked to see the mechanic who had serviced his airplane. The young man was sick with the agony of his mistake. Tears streamed down his face as Hoover approached. He had just caused the loss of a very expensive plane and could have caused the loss of three lives as well.

You can imagine Hoover's anger. One could anticipate the tongue-lashing that this proud and precise pilot would unleash for such carelessness. But Hoover didn't scold the mechanic; he didn't even criticize his gross negligence. Instead, he threw his big arm around the man's shoulder and said, "To show you I'm sure that you'll never do this again, I want you to service my F-51 tomorrow."

In life, sometimes mistakes are the by-product of extenuating circumstances. We don't always fail at work because of incompetence. We can fail because our hearts and minds are not engaged due to problems at home or elsewhere. The leader understands that mistakes and failures surface from all corners of life and, therefore, should be treated as isolated and redeemable instances rather than fatal flaws.

In an age where emerging leaders are skeptical of inauthentic leadership tactics, it is best to confront mistakes honestly while not using them as opportunities for condemnation. To many, passive-aggressive approaches or manipulative encounters with leaders diminish their view of that particular leader and make them cynical about their contribution to the task at hand or even the organization they serve. It is to your advantage to pull people out of their dejected state as quickly as possibly. Do so by calling out their mistakes quietly and returning them to a place of confidence and strength.

4
—

Ask Questions Instead of Giving Direct Orders

In the military, orders are a part of everyday operations. You receive orders and you are expected to follow them to a T. But when Captain D. Michael Abrashoff took command of the USS *Benfold,* a guided missile destroyer, he knew he was facing a challenge that would require a different approach.

The *Benfold* was not the top ship in the navy, not by far. The crew was sullen, morale was low, and most of the sailors on the ship were just biding their time until their discharge date. To add complexity to an already difficult leadership situation, the previous commander had not been well loved, so the crew was assessing their new leader with a harsh and critical eye.

But this was Captain Abrashoff's first sea command, and he was determined to do it well. His first step: learn about his crew. "It didn't take me long to realize that my young crew was smart, talented, and full of good ideas that frequently came to nothing because no one in charge had ever listened to them," wrote Captain Abrashoff in *It's Your Ship,* his leadership chronicles of his time aboard the *Benfold.*[1]

So Captain Abrashoff vowed to listen to his crew, but not just when they decided to speak up. He knew that if he wanted to turn the ship around, the ideas for how to do that had to come from the crew. And what better way to find out what their ideas were than to interview them? Captain Abrashoff interviewed five crew members a day until he had interviewed every crew member on board—approximately 310 of them. What did he learn?

That they wasted a lot of time on dreary chores, such as painting the ship six times a year. So Abrashoff found a way to replace all of the fasteners on the ship that caused rust streaks and a way to run many of the exterior panels through a special paint process. The ship didn't have to be painted again for almost two years, freeing up time for more valuable endeavors, such as advanced training. He learned that many of them had signed up for the navy as a way to pay for college. So he arranged for SAT testing on the ship and long-distance advanced placement courses for the crew. He found that many of them came from rough backgrounds and had led tough lives but also were very attached to their families, so he included family members as much as possible in the sailors' lives by sending birthday cards, letters of praise, and other important notes to parents and spouses. "I wanted to link our goals," wrote Captain Abrashoff, "so that they would see my priority of improving *Benfold* as an opportunity for them to apply their talents and give their jobs a real purpose."

What was the result of asking questions of his crew? A serious shift in morale, a greater willingness to push the limits of what was possible, and some of the highest testing rankings the navy had ever seen.

If Captain Abrashoff had stepped on board, issued a directive that the crew was to improve its rankings, and then outlined how that would happen, what might the result have been? We'll never know, but it is unlikely that the *Benfold* would have become the ship—or the leadership catalyst—it became.

Asking questions not only makes an order more palatable and reduces resentment, it often stimulates creativity and innovation in solving the problem at hand. People are more likely to follow a new path if they feel that they have been involved in shaping it.

The familial leaders of the Marriott organization were known for their intense devotion to inspecting Marriott hotels to ensure that they were well run. Bill Marriot Jr., in particular, "was constantly on the go, asking questions and paying close attention to the responses," writes Ed Fuller, the leader of Marriott International Lodging.

> In fact, sometimes he would be criticized for listening to too many people—and listening just as hard to frontline people as to senior executives. . . . His favorite question during his frontline visitations was, "What do you think?" It was his way of combating the tendency of employees to shy away from rocking the boat or passing on bad news to the boss.[2]

Bill Marriot Jr. was an enlightened leader who understood the negative power of the Mum Effect and how best to engage employees in making every Marriott property live up to his expectations.

While we understand that asking questions increases the engagement of those we hope to influence, many leaders don't take this route. Why? Because at times, asking questions can seem like a roundabout way to lead people to the answer you already have in your head. Why not just tell them? It would be more expedient.

People don't like to be ordered around, that's why.

Leaders are also reluctant to ask questions because they don't know what responses might result. What if the other person doesn't head in the direction you were intending? There is no way to overcome that possibility. Instead, leaders must think about it as an opportunity rather than as a risk. The answer you get may be better—likely will be better—than the one you already know.

When Ian Macdonald of Johannesburg, South Africa, the general manager of a small manufacturing plant specializing in precision machine parts, had the opportunity to accept a very large order, he was convinced that he could not meet the promised delivery date. The work already scheduled in the shop and the short completion time needed for this order made it seem impossible for him to accept the order.

Instead of pushing his people to accelerate their work and rush the order through, he called everybody together, explained the situation to them, and told them how much it would mean to the company and to them if they could make it possible to produce the order on time. Then he started asking questions: "Is there anything we can do to handle this order? Can anyone think of different ways to process it through the shop that will make it possible to take the order? Is there any way to adjust our hours or personnel assignments that would help?"

The employees came up with many ideas and insisted that he take the order. The order was accepted, produced, and delivered on time.

While it should not be the case, many leaders dread doing performance reviews. They know they have employees who need improvement, and they foresee a battle as they deliver criticism and the employees become increasingly defensive and sullen. These leaders need to take a different tack.

Most employees have a keen understanding of their own strengths and weaknesses. While some may be obtuse, most, if you ask, will tell you exactly what you are thinking. Many organizational psychologists recommend instituting a self-appraisal stage in the review process. Studies have shown that self-appraisals lead to reviews that are more satisfying for managers and employees and have a greater positive effect on performance.[3] Begin by giving the employee some questions to think about prior to the review: "What do you think you're exceptionally good at? What are your goals for the coming year? Where do you think you could improve your skills or abilities to help you meet those goals?"

Imagine beginning the meeting with a complete set of answers to these questions, answers that you don't have to deliver. At least 80 percent of the time, they will have come to the same conclusions you've arrived at and the conversation will be a much more positive one.

The wonderful thing about asking questions is that it can be effectively done in almost any medium. What if you sent a text or tweet to your team with a question about how to handle a recalcitrant client? Would that help employees who might be weak in this area reconsider their own methods or recognize that they don't have one? You can ask pretty powerful questions in 140 characters or less.

Questions allow you to create a conversation—in any medium—that can lead to a better place for all involved. And it allows everybody to feel that they were involved in shaping the outcome.

Wouldn't you rather be asked a question than be given an order?

5

Mitigate Fault

In the summer of 1941, Sergeant James Allen Ward was awarded the Victoria Cross for climbing out onto the wing of his Wellington bomber, thirteen thousand feet above Zuider Zee, to extinguish a fire in the starboard engine. Secured by only a rope around his waist, he managed to smother the fire and then return along the wing to the safety of the aircraft's cabin. Winston Churchill, an admirer as well as a performer of swashbuckling exploits, summoned the shy New Zealander to 10 Downing Street. Ward, struck dumb with awe in Churchill's presence, was unable to answer the prime minister's questions. Churchill surveyed the unhappy hero with some compassion. "You must feel very humble and awkward in my presence," he said.

"Yes sir," managed Ward.

"Then you can imagine how humble and awkward I feel in yours," said Churchill.[1]

With just a few words, Churchill moved Ward from a miserable fool to the hero he was. He mitigated fault and helped Ward save face.

Few of us take the time to consider how to let another save face. We ride roughshod over others' feelings, getting our own way, finding fault, issuing threats, criticizing a child or employee in front of others. We could offer a considerate word or two, take the other person's feelings into account, pull them aside—anything to alleviate the sting. Yet many of us don't take the time to do so.

For leaders, what does this insensitive behavior instill in those around us? Fear of failure. If we know we will be berated for our failures, possibly even publicly, will we take any risks in our work? Will we attempt to be innovative or creative? Will we speak up with ideas and opinions? Probably not.

Yet failure is an everyday part of our lives—at home, at work, in all of our endeavors. It is such a given that the venerable *Harvard Business Review* devoted its entire April 2011 issue to the subject. The cover heading and tagline? "The Failure Issue: How to Understand It, Learn from It, and Recover from It." Not one mention of avoiding it.

Of course, we intuitively know that failure is inevitable, so why can't we be more supportive when somebody is suffering through it?

An executive at a large media company was responsible for launching a new magazine. She spent a year's worth of time, effort, and resources trying to get the fledgling publication off the ground, but it never flew. The magazine had to be cancelled.

The CEO of the company, who could have fired or demoted the executive for the failure or who could have held her up as an example of what *not* to do, instead provided a psychological safety net, allowing the executive to save face. "The CEO stood up at a gathering of the firm's top executives and congratulated the failed executive for her courage and skill, for doing the wrong thing in the right way. He emphasized that the ill-fated decision wasn't just hers; senior management backed it, and the magazine failed despite great content and marketing," writes Robert Sutton in *Good Boss, Bad Boss*.[2]

What this CEO epitomized in his actions was a technique

that Sutton calls "forgive and remember," a critical path for learning from mistakes and changing behavior. The technique was first described by Charles L. Bosk in his book *Forgive and Remember: Managing Medical Failure*.[3] The goal is to help individuals achieve accountability while managing the existential problem of failure, a demoralizing inner battle for anyone. Isn't this the true responsibility of any leader? Because if the battle is lost, the individual will learn little from the mistake, have a diminished self-image, become fearful, and contribute less to the success of a company, a family, or any other organization.

Despite a leader's best efforts, those in his care will fail. And he will fail. Recognizing this and the inherent benefits failure may present can help us learn how to help others come through it and land positively and securely on the opposite shore. Great leaders tap the creative and innovative power of their teams by helping them save face before they've even failed.

Fiona Lee, Amy Edmundson, and Stefan Thomke conducted a study with 688 employees in a large health care organization during the rollout of a new data system that integrated and presented data from all departments and divisions within the organization. The employees received little training and were told to learn the system by experimenting with it.[3]

The findings? In departments where managers specifically told their teams that making mistakes was okay and didn't set up reward systems that penalized people who did make mistakes, experimentation with the system was much greater. In departments where managers were inconsistent in their messages or punished failure, even subtly, employees experimented with the system much less. In fact, lower-status employees in those departments didn't use the system at all because of their greater fear of failure. As you might expect, the employees who experimented the most with the new, more efficient system became the most proficient with it and used it regularly in their everyday work.

What the supportive managers were actually developing within their team members, even if only on a small scale, was resilience. Resilience, explains Martin P. Seligman, author and positive psychology pioneer, is the difference in the ways people respond to failure. In his books and other writings, he describes how some people bounce back from failure, learning and growing from the experience, while others languish, becoming self-critical and fearful of the future. Which would you rather foster in the people in your life?

Companies who recruit from the military have learned the value of resilience well; they recognize that people in the military are used to dealing with mistakes and failures, sometimes on an almost moment-by-moment basis, and moving forward purposefully despite them.

Donovan Campbell, author of *Joker One,* a memoir about his experience as a platoon leader in Iraq, is part of PepsiCo's elite Leadership Development Program. He explains the perspective he gained while commanding a platoon.

> In school you're rewarded for not making mistakes. And then you get out and get a job, and a lot of times you get promoted because you make very few mistakes. And so what you do is you develop a mindset that mistakes are to be avoided at all costs. What you learn in the military is that it doesn't matter how hard you try or how good you are. One, you will make mistakes; and two, sometimes events or the enemy or a changing situation will mean that you do not succeed, and in fact you fail. And you become comfortable with the idea.[4]

This mature approach to failure, as opposed to being frozen in a state of indecisiveness or inaction, is what we want from our employees and our leaders. Making it safe for them to fail is a sure way to ensure that they will more readily admit their mistakes (which is a key aspect of leadership we've explored), more quickly recover from them, more fully learn from them. As a leader, you will gain a more complete picture of their work and become a better coach and mentor for it.

So how do we create this type of environment? Charlene Li, in her important book *Open Leadership,* maps out five actions that leaders can take to instill organizational resilience within their teams:

- *Acknowledge that failure happens.* Leaders can acknowledge failures quickly when they happen, but they can also discuss with their teams the likelihood of failures occurring.
- *Encourage dialogue to foster trust.* Honestly discussing problems is the best way to learn from them and to trim the seedlings before they become fully grown catastrophes.
- *Separate the person from the failure.* Rather than saying "you failed," say "the project failed." In most cases, that is the truth. Amy Edmondson, Harvard professor and researcher, explored this point with executives. "When I ask executives to . . . estimate how many of the failures in their organizations are truly blameworthy, their answers are usually in single digits—perhaps 2% to 5%. But when I ask how many are treated as blameworthy, they say (after a pause or a laugh) 70% to 90%. The unfortunate consequence is that many failures go unreported and their lessons are lost."[5]
- *Learn from your mistakes.* Otherwise, they are lost opportunities for learning and for coaching.
- *Create a risk-taking and failure system.* Being methodical about how we approach risk and failure can help mitigate some of the emotional responses to it.

Why go to these lengths? Alberto Alessi, the great Italian designer, described his company's approach to design as an effort to find the borderline between what is possible and what is not possible and design along it. The best designs are those that fall right on the edge of the borderline, just this side of possible. That is the space of innovation, the space where we test our talents and grow as individuals. Of course, hugging the line means that you will often flop over it—you will fall into the realm of the impossible and fail. But what a glorious failure it will be, and who knows what might be learned from it. Famed vacuum cleaner designer Sir Richard Dyson produced more than five thousand prototypes before bringing his first product to market.

What we must remember when faced with a person who has made a mistake is that how he handles it is dependent on the support he receives while living through the tough moment and learning from it. A primary difference between ordinary and extraordinary people is how they perceive and respond to failure. A good leader can influence which camp we fall into.

Now, there are mistakes and then there are "mistakes." Some mistakes come about from minor lapses in judgment, from inexperience, from the need for coaching. These are actual mistakes. Others come about from recklessness, greed, a lack of concern for others' well-being, and a desire to elevate oneself at the expense of others. In these instances, it's highly likely that the person at fault actually feels no remorse, no sense of accountability. Is it appropriate to help such an individual save face? Possibly not. If the mistake and attitude are severe enough, it's likely that helping the other person save face would just exacerbate the problem. In these instances, it's best to keep public comments to a minimum and use private conversations to address the severity of the issue as deftly as possible.

Other than creating an environment in which people are not

pilloried for their mistakes when part of a larger whole, Charlene Li's advice can be transferred to situations when we should help an individual save face to recover from a minor error, oversight, or gaffe.

- Acknowledge that a mistake was made, but do it gently. Pretending that nothing happened certainly meets the "forgive" criteria, but it seems a little disingenuous when the error was blatant.
- Recognize and address your own role, even if minor.
- Focus on what was gained.
- When appropriate to do so without making others culpable, address the issue from a broad perspective.

Imagine that you are at a function and are introduced to somebody you've met before, but he clearly doesn't remember you. You could say, "We've met before," throwing his error in his face. Or you could say, "Oh, hello, Mark. It's nice to see you again. Did I see you at the Better Business Bureau lunch last month? It was a great networking event, although there were so many people, it was a bit overwhelming."

Today, our faults, missteps, and outright failures are so much more public than they once were. When an employee makes a mistake, it's not surprising when a customer starts blogging about it, posts the experience on her Facebook page, or shoots off a quick email tirade to the CEO of the company. The employee is already in a position to feel humiliated and fearful. Why make it worse? Allowing others to save face is crucial in the digital age.

Of course, helping someone save face is sometimes more difficult to do because his failures have been broadcast. It is important to maintain strict discipline in terms of what you write in emails. An email accidentally sent to the wrong person or hacked and posted on a blog may not only cause embarrassment but also ruin somebody's professional reputation. If you need to discuss a mistake or gaffe that somebody made, it's best to do it in person or over the phone. Save your written communication for praise and constructive advice.

While it's important to help others weather their failures gracefully, helping a customer or potential customer save face can be useful as a business tactic. Wolfgang Schmidt explained how his company, Rubbermaid, uses the technique to win new customers:

> We do get complaints. About half those complaints come about as a result of a consumer buying a product, thinking it's ours, but it's a competitor's product. So the consumer writes to us. Our policy is simply to write a personal letter and say, "We can understand how you made the mistake because we have these competitors who copy our products. You made an honest mistake, but we would like for you to see directly the difference in value. So try one of ours for free." We send them our replacement product for whatever it is they complained about. And we think that's a wonderful way to communicate very credibly the story of Rubbermaid value.[6]

Even if the other person is wrong, we only destroy ego by causing someone to lose face. We do nothing to change his or her behavior.

On the other hand, when we mitigate fault, we not only save the other person's psyche, we build confidence and trust into our relationship with that person. Save someone's face once and your influence with him rises. Save his face every time you can, and there is practically nothing he won't do for you.

6

Magnify Improvement

One bright day in 2010, the hotel company Best Western created a special Facebook page. Visitors flocked to it. Hundreds of messages were posted to the wall.

> "Wallace makes weary travelers feel like they're coming home! The best thing about the hotel lobby is his smile."
>
> "Wallace is the best. We love going back just to visit with him!"
>
> "Upon leaving, the kids asked when we were coming back to see Wallace!"
>
> "I may pass him in the lobby or the hall fifteen times in a visit, and every time, he has a great big smile and something fun to say. He is one of the greatest parts of my visits!"
>
> "We should all relate to one another as Wallace does. If he ever has a bad day, you wouldn't know it."
>
> "In all of my travels, I've never encountered anyone more kind and helpful, more eager to make a guest feel welcome."
>
> "My day is always made brighter by seeing Wallace. His always warm welcome, his knowledge of the city, his kindness and professionalism, and that terrific smile make my stay so enjoyable. . . . He has a special gift for connecting with people."

Who is this Wallace? Wallace Pope—Chicago native, single dad, longtime employee of Best Western River North Hotel, and a man who loves helping others.

When Wallace was nominated for the Stars of the Industry award from the Illinois Hotel and Lodging Association, Best Western was determined to show its pride and support—and to help him win.[1] So the company created a Facebook page called "Wallace Should Win" and encouraged visitors to the hotel to go to the page and share their stories of Wallace's customer service skills. The page had 2,722 visits within the first week. Heartfelt stories of love and support poured in from the hotel's customers. Wallace's genuine kindness and his ability to improve customers' travel and personal outlook were lauded again and again. And while Wallace didn't win the award, the praise and encouragement he gained from the Facebook page was far more meaningful than a plaque.

Praise and encouragement: the two essential elements of motivating any person to fulfill their potential, to improve, or to tackle change. Yet it's difficult for many of us to recognize the efforts of those around us.

Dr. Gerald Graham was curious about what managers could do to better motivate employees. So he surveyed fifteen hundred employees, and the results were rather shocking:

- 58 percent reported that they seldom if ever received praise from their manager
- 76 percent reported that they seldom if ever received written thanks
- 81 percent reported that they seldom if ever received praise in public

And yet praise from a manager, written thanks, and public praise were three of the top five motivators among the surveyed employees.[2]

These results were from 1982. Decades later, things haven't changed all that much. Employees who receive frequent praise are still more productive, and organizations in which employees receive frequent praise are universally more successful. It's one of the twelve indicators of success that Marcus Buckingham and Curt Koffman outline in *First, Break All the Rules*, indicators based on extensive Gallup Organization research. Yet managers are still notoriously bad at delivering praise.

We all crave appreciation; we all desire to feel important. And when we have improved in some way or performed well, receiving praise sends a clear message that others have noticed and that it makes a difference. This is true at work, at home, at school, in our communities. One of the basic psychological tenets of human behavior is that we persist in behaviors for which we are praised; those behaviors that are not positively recognized are likely to fall by the wayside.

The Center for Management and Organization Effectiveness offers the following advice for praising those around you:[3]

1. "Deliver praise from your heart." Be genuine and sincere.
2. "Deliver praise as soon as possible." Don't wait for the next meeting, performance review, family meal, or church gathering. By then, the person's own joy at the success has dissipated, and you've lost an opportunity to amplify that joy.
3. "Make praise specific." A simple thank-you is not praise; it is politeness. To feel that their efforts are heading them down the path you want them to go, people need to know exactly what you valued in their effort.
4. "Praise people publicly." In this era of social technology, praising publicly gets easier every day, so there is no real

excuse not to do it. Best Western certainly did. Today you don't have to wait for the next quarterly meeting to recognize a job well done.

We should strive to praise as often as possible. Most of us don't have to struggle to find opportunities to do so; we simply have to take advantage of the opportunities that exist every day.

Captain Abrashoff of the USS *Benfold* understood the power of praise better than most:

> Most of my young sailors came from hardscrabble backgrounds and had struggled to make it into the Navy. I put myself in their parents' shoes and imagined how they would feel if they got letters from their kids' commanding officer, and I imagined how the kids would feel when their parents told them. I began writing letters to the parents, especially when their sons or daughters did something I could honestly praise. When the letters arrived, the parents invariably called their children to say how proud they were of them.[4]

One sailor was part of a team that had performed very well, but was himself not a star. Captain Abrashoff recognized that praising his accomplishments as part of a team would give this sailor the boost he most likely needed. So he sent the letter of praise to the young man's parents. Two weeks later, the sailor knocked on Captain Abrashoff's door with tears streaming down his face.

"I just got a call from my father, who all my life told me I'm a failure. This time, he said he's just read your letter, and he wanted to congratulate me and say how proud he was of me. It's the first time in my entire life he's actually encouraged me."

Obviously this was a powerful moment for this young man.

How do you think it affected his view of what he could achieve and his level of devotion to the success of his team?

Praise, while powerful and necessary, also implies evaluation against some standard. What great leaders and those with influence recognize is that the rest of the time, we must use encouragement. "Praise is given only when one achieves 'good' results; encouragement can be given any time, even when things go poorly."[5]

That is the essence of encouragement—showing your belief in the talents, skills, and inherent abilities of another person because she exists, regardless of how things are going right now.

Being encouraging requires a special attitude. When you look at another person, rather than seeing her faults, you need to be able to see her strengths and possibilities, what she is capable of. Insincere encouragement, without the strength of your genuine faith in the other person, only belittles her efforts.

What does encouragement foster in the other person? Psychological hardiness—the ability to weather the stressful and anxiety-inducing challenges that we encounter every day, to face those challenges and move forward in spite of them, to pick ourselves up and keep going, keep trying. It is the hallmark of positive, successful people.

Encouragement provides motivation, and finding ways to motivate is a huge struggle for leaders in all areas of life. The primary cause of that struggle? Many of us don't take the time to consider what actually motivates people. We often assume that people want material rewards, that the carrot-and-stick approach is the best approach—but this is rarely the case. People are genuinely more motivated by personal and social encouragement than by material rewards.

Through his research on healthy marriages and families,

author and psychologist Jon Carlson defined some essential practices that we can use to create an encouraging environment:[6]

1. Make healthy relationships a priority. Respect and positive communication are two key elements of making that happen.
2. Practice encouragement daily. Don't wait until somebody has stumbled on the path toward a goal. Recognize every effort and every improvement, even if it is slight, to let them know that your faith in them is unwavering.
3. Be inclusive. For instance, include others in your decision-making process whenever possible; it shows your faith in their sound judgment.
4. Don't let conflicts fester. When we're in conflict mode, it's easy to slip into discouraging or belittling dialogue. Compare "I think you can do it" and "Looks like we have problem—what should we do about it?" with "Just let me take care of this" or "I told you to be careful."
5. Have fun!

Clarence M. Jones, a Carnegie Institute instructor, told how encouragement and making faults seem easy to correct completely changed the life of his son:

My son David, who was then fifteen years old, came to live with me in Cincinnati. He had led a rough life. In 1958 his head was cut open in a car accident, leaving a very bad scar on his forehead. In 1960 his mother and I were divorced and he moved to Dallas, Texas, with his mother. He had spent most of his school years in special classes for slow learners. Possibly because of the scar, school administrators had decided he was brain-injured and could not function at a normal level. He was two years behind his age group, so he was only in the seventh grade. Yet he did not know his multiplication tables, added on his fingers, and could barely read.

There was one positive point. He loved to work on radio and TV sets. He wanted to become a TV technician. I encouraged this and pointed out that he needed math to qualify for the training. I decided to help him become proficient in this subject. We obtained four sets of flash cards: multiplication, division, addition, and subtraction. As we went through the cards, we put the correct answers in a discard stack. When David missed one, I gave him the correct answer and then put the card in the repeat stack until there were no more cards left. I made a big deal out of each card he got right, particularly if he had missed it previously.

Each night we would go through the repeat stack until there were no cards left. Each night we timed the exercise with a stopwatch. I promised him that when he could get all the cards correct in eight minutes with no incorrect answers, we would quit doing it every night. This seemed an impossible goal to David. The first night it took 52 minutes, the second night, 48, then 45, 44, 41, then under 40 minutes. We celebrated each reduction. I'd call in my wife and we would both hug him and we'd all dance a jig. At the end of the month he was doing all the cards perfectly in less than eight minutes. When he made a small improvement he would ask to do it again. He had made the fantastic discovery that learning was easy and fun.

Naturally his grades in algebra took a jump. It is amazing how much easier algebra is when you can multiply. He astonished himself by bringing home a B in math. That had never happened before. Other changes came with almost unbelievable rapidity. His reading improved rapidly, and he began to use his natural talents in drawing. Later in the school year his science teacher assigned him to develop an exhibit. He chose to develop a highly complex series of models to demonstrate the effect of levers. It required skill not only in drawing and model making but in applied mathematics. The exhibit took first prize in his school's science fair and was entered in the city competition and won third prize for the entire city of Cincinnati.

That did it. Here was a kid who had flunked two grades, who had been told he was "brain-damaged," who had been called "Frankenstein" by his classmates and told his brains must have leaked out of the cut on his head. Suddenly he discovered he could really learn and accomplish things. The result? From the last quarter of the eighth grade all the way through high school, he never failed to make the honor roll; in high school he was elected to the national honor society. Once he found learning was easy, his whole life changed.

Tell someone that you have total faith in his ability to accomplish a goal and encourage him by highlighting all of the skills he possesses that will help him along the way, and he will practice until the dawn comes in the window in order to excel.

Remember, abilities wither under criticism and blossom under encouragement. Magnify improvement and you maximize others' talents.

7

Give Others a Fine Reputation to Live Up To

Benjamin Zander was tired—tired of watching his conservatory students, so anxious about the grading of their performances in his class, take a safe approach to their music education. In the top tiers of the arts world, bitter competition can define the talent development process. He considered abandoning grades altogether, but that presented a host of challenges, not the least of which was getting the head of the school to approve such a radical move.

Instead, he decided he would give each student an A—on the very first day of class.

Upon meeting his new and nervous students, he would say, "Each student in this class will get an A for the course. However, there is one requirement that you must fulfill to earn this grade: Some time during the next two weeks, you must write me a letter dated next May . . . and in this letter you are to tell, in as much detail as you can, the story of what will have happened to you by next May that is in line with this extraordinary grade."

He instructed the students to think of themselves in the future, looking back on all that they had done to earn such an illustrious grade. They were to discuss insights, milestones, and even competitions won. But Zander wanted more than a surface analysis. "I am especially interested in the person you will have become by next May. I am interested in the attitude, feelings, and worldview of that person who will have done all she wished to do or become everything he wanted to be," he would say to them.[1]

What did he get from his students? Consider the following letter from a young trombonist:

Dear Mr. Z:

Today the world knows me. That drive of energy and intense emotion that you saw twisting and dormant inside me, yet, alas, I could not show in performance or conversation, was freed tonight in a program of new music composed for me. . . . The concert ended and no one stirred. A pregnant quiet. Sighs: and then applause that drowned my heart's throbbing.

I might have bowed—I cannot remember now. The clapping sustained such that I thought I might make my debut complete and celebrate the shedding of

the mask and skin
that I had constructed
to hide within
by improvising on my own melody as an
encore—unaccompanied. What followed is
something of a blur. I forgot technique,
pretension, tradition, schooling, history—
truly even the audience.
What came from my trombone
I wholly believe, was my own

Voice.
Laughter, smiles,
a frown, weeping
Tuckerspirit
did sing.

—Tucker Dulin

Over the ten months of his course, Zander watched his students transform themselves in astounding ways. He calls his approach "giving an A." In his book *The Art of Possibility,* coauthored with his wife, Rosamund Stone Zander, he has this to say about its potential to foster greatness in an individual:

> An A can be given to anyone in any walk of life—to a waitress, to your employer, to your mother-in-law, to the members of the opposite team, and to the other drivers in traffic. When you give an A, you find yourself speaking to people not from a place of measuring how they stack up against your standards, but from a place of respect that gives them room to realize themselves. . . . This A is not an expectation to live up to, but a possibility to live into.[2]

What a magical perspective to assume in an often cynical world.

Coaches, mentors, leaders, and parents often find that people live up to our expectations of them, no matter how diminished those expectations are. If a man feels unimportant or disrespected, he will have little motivation for improving himself. So why not create a vision of him that embodies everything you know he is capable of achieving, as well as everything you don't know about his possibilities? You will rarely be disappointed.

Paige Ann Michelle McCabe's mother described her own adventures in creating a big-girl reputation for her daughter:

Four-year-old Paige Ann Michelle McCabe was sitting on one of our kitchen stools when she heard me tell her six-year-old brother, Brandon, that it was now his responsibility to set the table each night before dinner. Paige looked hopeful and almost teary. "What am I big enough to do now, Mummy? What can I do 'cause I'm big too?" Not wanting to break her little heart or deflate her ego, I searched quickly for something that she could take responsibility for.

An idea crept into my head just in time. "Paige Ann Michelle," I announced triumphantly, "now that you are four years old, and old enough to make proper choices, you are responsible for choosing your clothes for the next day. Each night before you take a bath, you should get your clothes out of your drawer, and put them on the bed ready to wear in the morning when you wake up."

The house was a flurry of activity. Brandon was zooming around setting the table, and Paige ran straight to her room, where I could hear drawers and cupboards hurriedly opening and closing. About ten seconds later she ran out to report her success. "Look, Mummy, I did it, I got them out! Come and see, come and see!" Sure enough, the clothes were laid out on the bed, ready to go. I told her how proud I was, now that she was growing up and had her very own job to do, and she beamed.

The next morning, a miracle occurred in the McCabe house.

Usually, Mummy has to coax a grumpy Paige out of bed, and getting her dressed is difficult, to say the least. If I choose a blue skirt, she wants to wear red pants. If I choose a white shirt with butterflies, she wants to wear the purple shirt with flowers on it. Finally when I give in and tell her to choose, she takes forever. Paige stays grumpy and I end up frustrated.

But not that morning. "Look what I am wearing, Mummy!" she said. She had got herself dressed before I had asked her to! I kissed her proudly and told her how happy I was with her choices. It was morning and Paige Ann Michelle McCabe was happy. What a difference that made!

Paige Ann Michelle McCabe had lived up to the fine reputation of a grown-up four-year-old that had been bestowed upon her.

To change somebody's behavior, change the level of respect she receives by giving her a fine reputation to live up to. Act as though the trait you are trying to influence is already one of the person's outstanding characteristics.

8

Stay Connected on Common Ground

The employees of a manufacturing company had been on strike for six months when a labor contract was finally agreed upon. The terms, however, were less than what the employees had originally asked for. While the employees did return to work, tensions were running high on both sides. The working environment was toxic. How could they get past the animosity and move forward?

In *Crucial Conversations,* authors Kerry Patterson, Joseph Grenny, Ron McMillan, and Al Switzer described how they worked with the two groups to build bridges. They instructed each group to spend time considering their goals for the company and to write them out on poster-sized paper. Each group spent two hours discussing their goals, then wrote the goals on the paper and posted it on the wall in the room they were in. The coaches then asked the teams to switch rooms and to review the other group's goals with the purpose of finding at least some morsel of common ground.

What do you think happened?

When the two groups returned to the meeting room, they

were amazed. Their goals were almost identical: "a profitable company, stable and rewarding jobs, high-quality products, and a positive impact on the community."[1]

While this revelation didn't erase the past, it provided each group with a new perspective on the other. They learned something about each other that would make it easier to reach more positive outcomes in the future.

Why is common ground so important? For a leader to effectively influence another's attitude or behavior, he needs to overcome any potential resistance by making the person feel glad to do what is being asked. We aren't talking about manipulation or mind control here. If you consider what the other's goals are and how to connect your goals to hers, you will create a win-win situation that will make everybody glad.

It is amazing how simple it is today to find a connection with another when we take the time to. If you go on an interview or a sales call, wouldn't you spend time researching the company, discovering its vision, its stated goals, its values? All of this is information that many companies post front and center on their websites. And many go much further, posting employee bios, press releases, and updated information on their blogs.

Yet we often don't take the time to make these same inroads with those in our lives, those standing right in front of us, even though it is just as easy. Ask people what they did over the weekend, what they hope to do for their next vacation, or what books they've recently read, and you'll discover something compelling and revealing about their goals, their dreams. And if you're connected with them online, it may be even easier.

Six degrees to Kevin Bacon is an interesting pop culture phenomenon, but it's actually a fantastic way to think about those you want to influence. When you expand the translation to include common interests, common experiences, common goals, the truth is that we are only one degree away from anyone. To be influential with others, to make them happy to do what it is we would like them to do, we simply have to find that one degree that connects us.

One student of the Dale Carnegie Training Institute in Germany discovered that taking the bold path of simply writing to those people she wanted to learn more about—to possibly find that one degree of connection—produced wondrous results.

> As I was very shy, I decided to write emails to the people I was interested in. I researched and found the addresses of very famous and well-known people and started to ask them questions about their backgrounds, such as how they got started in their businesses and what was important to them personally.
>
> Two weeks later I received a two-paged letter from the German president Johannes Rau, who answered my questions. Six weeks later I received another letter. It was a big envelope, and a book was enclosed that would answer my questions. It was sent to me by His Holiness the Dalai Lama.

What did this person learn? If you make the effort, people—all people, even those who seem unapproachable—will tell you their stories, their motivations and their goals.

One night, Dana White, the president of the Ultimate Fighting Championship sports league, accidentally tweeted his direct phone number to more than one million fans, who retweeted it to untold numbers of people. The fans began calling within minutes. A leader less focused on making his customers happy would have called the phone company and had his number changed immediately. But that is not what Dana White did.

For more than an hour and a half, he took the calls that came in and talked to the fans. They loved it.

It was a fortunate mistake, and Dana White learned a lot from it. He learned that talking to fans was valuable, and the PR company that helps manage UFC's online presence learned that they had a new opportunity to "provide value to fans, when, where and how they want to receive it."[2]

Now Dana White has a dedicated line that he uses to take calls from fans. It's posted on all of his social media outlets. When he has time, he lets them know he's ready to talk, and the phone starts ringing.

His accidental ninety minutes on the phone with UFC fans from all over the world was no gimmick, and that is key to ultimate fighting being the fastest-growing sport in the world, according to Mashable's Greg Ferenstein.[3] White has been passionate about connecting with fans through social media from the start, and relied on the grassroots support of his fans when major media refused to cover UFC events. When he hired Digital Royalty to grow UFC's online presence and train the fighters in social media techniques, he told the fighters, "I want you to tweet your asses off!" The secret of his success in connecting with his fans: he is brutally honest and frank.

To prove the power of this connection to a companion, White left a restaurant and walked to a nearby gas station at eleven-thirty at night. He tweeted his location. Within three minutes, there were about one hundred fans there.

In his analysis of Dana White's efforts, Greg Ferenstein wrote, "Transparency, outreach and openness are now more important than ever, as social media allows fans to subvert traditional channels and voice their opinions directly. White is willing to meet them halfway, foregoing false showmanship in order to genuinely connect with fans."

While social media is a great tool for learning what drives

somebody, it is only a tool. What leaders need to foster within themselves is a genuine desire to ascertain the answer and then to act on the information, a desire that many failed executives undermine, both knowingly and unknowingly. Of this depreciated desire among many high-powered executives, *Derailed* author Dr. Tim Irwin concludes:

> Just as humility seems to be at the epicenter of leadership effectiveness, arrogance is commonly at the root of a leader's undoing . . . and ours. . . . Arrogance takes many forms. The most rudimentary is the self-centered focus that fosters a belief that I am central to the viability of the organization, the department or the team. The resulting dismissiveness of others' contributions is inevitable. When arrogance blossoms into hubris, a sense of entitlement results. "This place can't function without me, and I deserve special perks." Arrogant leaders also seem to eschew feedback so beneficial to any leader. They become truth-starved.[4]

A contrasting approach is found in Yvon Chouinard, co-founder (with his wife, Malinda) of Patagonia and author of *Let My People Go Surfing*. Yvon is proud of the fact that Patagonia hires the intensely independent—people who "would be considered unemployable in a typical company," he's been told by organizational consultants. While he revels in his independent-minded employees, it also presents a management challenge: how to build a collaborative unit all focused on the same goals.

One tool he uses is the design of the offices. "No one has a private office in our company and everyone works in open rooms with no doors or separations [including Yvon and Malinda]. What we lose in 'quiet thinking space' is more than made up for with better communication and an egalitarian atmosphere."[5]

Now take it a step further and consider Admiral Janitorial

Services, the fictional company described in Matthew Kelly's *The Dream Manager*. Turnover is high and costly, not surprising for a company staffed by transient workers. What to do? First, find out their biggest struggle. The company assumes that the biggest cause of turnover is pay, but when it surveys the employees it discovers that their biggest struggle is transportation. Many rely on public transportation, which is spotty and even dangerous at night. What should the leaders of the company do? They provide shuttle service. It's costly, but what they save in turnover costs more than makes up for it. Employees stay twice as long, sick days have dropped, and morale is higher.

Still, the leaders know they could do better. What really makes people leave? they wonder. The jobs are dead-end ones, not dream-fulfilling positions, and everybody knows it. The leaders decide that they can't fix that, but they can find ways to help employees move closer to their dreams while they work for Admiral. So they ask the employees, "What are your dreams?" Surprisingly (or maybe not), the employees tell them. Now the company has powerful information—and it uses it to help the employees achieve their dreams. One employee wants to learn Spanish; another, who happens to be a Spanish speaker, wants to teach. So the company connects them.

Yes, this story is fictional, but does the example seem extreme?

Why shouldn't we know what our colleagues, coworkers, friends, and family members dream? How powerful that information would be. How central that information would be for sustaining a course whereby you and those in your sphere of influence achieve what is desired.

Do you know what motivates the people around you? There are simple ways to find out. And once you have the information, it is a simple process to link your desired outcomes with their goals:

1. Be sincere. Do not promise anything that you cannot deliver.
2. Be empathetic. Ask yourself what it is the other person really wants.
3. Consider the benefits the person will receive from doing what you suggest.
4. Match those benefits to the other person's wants.
5. When you make your request, put it in a form that will convey to the other person the idea that he personally will benefit.

The more you know of others and the more they know of you, the easier it will be to find common ground on which to base all future creativity and collaboration. Staying connected with customers in the digital world, says Richard Branson, the Virgin Group mogul recently voted Most Influential British Business Figure, is keeping many executives awake at night.

> How companies adapt to this energetic and sometimes chaotic world will define their future success. The website, Facebook page, blog and Twitter feed are no longer add-ons to a business's communication budget: They should be central to its marketing strategy, and used in coordination with other marketing efforts.[6]

The key, says Branson, is not defaulting your digital media into mere transactional mode; instead, open them wide for ongoing communication as well. We now live in a connected world where the idea of companies and customers being instantly and constantly in touch is not an exception; it's the expectation.

"The rise of social media," writes Branson,

has presented exciting challenges and caused us to question our usual ways of doing business. . . . To succeed, such efforts must be supported from the top. David Cush, CEO of Virgin America, freed up the management of these social media channels from the company's classic hierarchy. His social media team is made up of 20-somethings who have been given broad guidelines and then let loose.

These digital natives at Virgin have employed Facebook and Twitter as part of the company's communication strategy. This open digital connection allowed for a unique connection opportunity that flowed into a successful marketing campaign.

Many West Coast animal shelters were bursting at the seams with Chihuahuas, and something needed to be done to give the little dogs a better chance to find good homes. The American Society for the Prevention of Cruelty to Animals intervened, contacting Virgin America and asking if the airline would help fly several dogs from San Francisco to New York. Virgin immediately agreed and even volunteered crew members to accompany the small passengers.

Virgin's digital team promoted this story through all their communication channels. "It went viral," explains Branson, "and also sparked the interest of the traditional media—drawing attention to the ASPCA and Virgin Atlantic's efforts to help. We then used the story as the basis of a very successful online sale on flights to Mexico."

The traditional roles of advertising, marketing, and customer relations have changed. So too has the role of today's leader. In digital time and space, with open access and frequent communication, the perfunctory principles of corporate activity have largely broken down and been replaced by the basic principles of human relations. If you don't know how to win friends and influence people in a genuine and positive manner today, not only will you have trouble keeping pace in a marketplace ruled by the consumer, you will also have trouble keeping your people employed.

Long gone are the days when leaders can lord it over their reports from behind closed doors in top-floor offices accessible only by private elevators. In truth, those days never existed where effective leadership is concerned—not in 1936 and not now. Today, with full-time connectivity as the norm, the consequences of remote leadership are more palpable. Physical proximity is not the main issue. Relational proximity is.

While an individual can only occasionally maintain a productive, progressive relationship without a reasonable measure of physical presence, no person in the world—especially a leader—can maintain progressive influence without relational proximity.

It is true that the world is now open for business, but your first task remains the business of humanity. The greatest endeavors are and always will be interdependent and interactive. In the end, the art of winning friends and influencing people in the digital age is summed up in the activity of connecting and staying connected on common ground.

Notes

WHY CARNEGIE'S ADVICE STILL MATTERS

1. James Thurber, "Friends, Romans, Countrymen, Lend Me Your Ear-muffs," in *Lanterns and Lances* (New York: Harper & Brothers, 1961).

2. "Leading Thoughts: Quotes on Communication," *Leadership Now* (blog), www.leadershipnow.com/communicationquotes.html.

3. Thanks to Building Champions corporate coach, Steve Scanlon, for his insightful phrasing on this Carnegie principle. His insights and services can be found here: www.buildingchampions.com or www.realityand hope.com.

4. Jesus, while admonishing the two-faced religious leaders of the Galilean cities, as recorded in Matthew 12:34.

5. Antoine de Saint-Exupéry, French writer, poet, and aviator. The quote is widely attributed to him, while the specific source remains unknown.

6. Shakespeare, *Macbeth*, act 5, scene 5, lines 19–28.

7. Luc de Clapiers, marquis de Vauvenargues, *The réflections and maxims of Luc de Clapiers, marquis of Vauvenargues* (London: H. Milford, 1940).

8. Dr. John Andrew Holmes, *Wisdom in Small Doses* (Lincoln, NE: University Publishing Company, 1927).

9. Tom Butler-Bowdon, *50 Self-Help Classics* (London: Nicholas Brealey, 2004).

10. "The 2010 TIME 100," *Time*, http://www.time.com/time/specials/packages/0,28757,1984685,00.html.

11. Lynn Hirschberg, "The Self-Manufacture of Megan Fox," *New York Times Magazine*, November 11, 2009.

PART 1: ESSENTIALS OF ENGAGEMENT

CHAPTER 1: BURY YOUR BOOMERANGS

1. ThinkExist, http://thinkexist.com/quotes/adolf_hitler; http://thinkexist.com/quotes/martin_luther_king,_jr.

2. Lori Culbert, "Ex-Doctor Fined for Facebook Comments," *Vancouver Sun,* November 20, 2010.

3. "Liverpool's Ryan Babel Fined £10,000 for Twitter Post," BBC, January 17, 2011, http://news.bbc.co.uk/sport2/hi/football/teams/l/liverpool/9363567.stm.

4. Ben Dirs, "How Twitter Changed the Rules," BBC, January 17, 2011, www.bbc.co.uk/blogs/bendirs/2011/01/twitter_blog.html.

5. Proofpoint website, www.proofpoint.com/outbound.

6. Catharine Smith and Craig Kanalley, "Fired over Facebook: 13 Posts That Got People Canned," *Huffington Post,* July 26, 2010, www.huffingtonpost.com/2010/07/26/fired-over-facebook-posts_n_659170.html#s115707&title=Swiss_Woman_Caught.

7. "Waitress Fired for Facebook Comment," May 17, 2010, UPI, www.upi.com/Odd_News/2010/05/17/Waitress-fired-for-Facebook-comment/UPI-39861274136251.

8. Matthew J. Darnell, "Eagles Fire Employee for Calling Them 'Retarded' on Facebook," Yahoo Sports, March 9, 2009, http://sports.yahoo.com/nfl/blog/shutdown_corner/post/Eagles-fire-employee-for-calling-them-retarted-?urn=nfl-146801.

9. "Farm Boy Workers Fired After Chat Site Critiques," *Ottawa Citizen,* January 18, 2007, www.canada.com/ottawacitizen/news/business/story.html?id=8b2bf234–06b4–419f-b5f7–35e3dc338637.

10. *Baseball's Steroid Era,* www.baseballssteroidera.com.

11. "Jesse Jackson Apologizes for Comments Critical of Obama," *Political Ticker* (blog), CNN, July 9, 2008, http://politicalticker.blogs.cnn.com/2008/07/09/jesse-jackson-apologizes-for-comments-critical-of-obama.

12. Jesus, in the famous Sermon on the Mount, Matthew 7:2.

13. Philip Yancey, *Soul Survivor* (Colorado Springs: Galilee Trade, 2003).

14. "Books: Orthodoxologist," *Time,* October 11, 1943, www.time.com/time/magazine/article/0,9171,774701–3,00.html.

15. Gilbert Keith Chesterton, *The Autobiography of G. K. Chesterton* (San Francisco: Ignatius Press, 2006).

16. "G. K. Chesterton," *Wikipedia,* http://en.wikipedia.org/wiki/G._K._Chesterton.

CHAPTER 2: AFFIRM WHAT'S GOOD

1. ThinkExist, http://thinkexist.com/quotation/thought_is_the_blossom-language_the_bud-action/177845.html.

2. *The King's Speech*, Weinstein Company and UK Film Council, 2010.

3. A famous parable told by Jesus as described in Matthew 18:12–14 and Luke 15:3–7.

4. Clifton Fadiman and André Bernard, eds., *Bartlett's Book of Anecdotes* (New York: Little, Brown, 2000), 13.

5. Rick Warren, *The Purpose-Driven Life* (Grand Rapids, MI: Zondervan, 2002).

6. Ralph Waldo Emerson, *The Conduct of Life* (1860), VIII: Beauty.

7. The line is cited by Ralph Waldo Emerson in his essay "Goethe; or, the Writer" in *Representative Men* (University Press of the Pacific, August 1, 2001) and attributed to or at least inspired by German playwright and poet Johann Wolfgang von Goethe.

8. Ed Fuller, *You Can't Lead with Your Feet on the Desk* (Hoboken, NJ: Wiley, 2011), 45–46.

9. In an interview with the writer between November 2010 and January 2011.

CHAPTER 3: CONNECT WITH CORE DESIRES

1. Josh Quittner with reporting by Rebecca Winters, "Apple's New Core," *Time,* January 14, 2002.

2. In an interview with the writer on February 14, 2011.

3. Richard Norton Smith, "The Reagan Revelation: At 100, Why He Still Matters," *Time,* February 7, 2011, www.time.com/time/nation/article/0,8599,2044565,00.html.

4. Michael Scherer and Michael Duffy, "The Role Model," *Time,* February 7, 2011.

5. Smith, "The Reagan Revelation."

6. Harry Allen Overstreet, *Influencing Human Behavior* (New York: W. W. Norton, 1925).

7. Todd Duncan, *Killing the Sale* (Nashville: Nelson Business, 2004).

8. Theodore Zeldin, *Conversation: How Talk Can Change Our Lives* (London: Harvill Press, 1998).

9. Duncan, *Killing the Sale.* The descriptions are slightly revised with permission.

10. David Shaner, *The Seven Arts of Change* (New York: Union Square Press, 2010).

11. As told by a former presidential speechwriter who was interviewed for this book.

PART 2: SIX WAYS TO MAKE A LASTING IMPRESSION

CHAPTER 1: TAKE INTEREST IN OTHERS' INTERESTS

1. An inscription on the monument of a Newfoundland dog: "A Memorial to Boatswain," by Lord Byron, Newstead Abbey, November 30, 1808.

2. Matthew 23:12.

3. A special thanks to Steve Beecham and his refreshing business treatise *Bass-Ackward Business* (Alpharetta, GA: Home Town Marketing, 2009), for this particular phrasing.

4. From a conversation between a former presidential speechwriter and Andrew Sullivan, as relayed to the writer.

5. From Anne Rice's website: www.annerice.com.

6. Ibid.

7. Anne Rice's Facebook page, www.facebook.com/pages/Anne-Rice/112356685446315.

8. Beecham, *Bass-Ackward Business.*

9. Ibid.

10. Kris Ruby, "20 Best-Branded Women on Twitter," *Forbes,* August 5, 2010, www.forbes.com/2010/08/05/twitter-followers-social-media-marketing-online-community-forbes-woman-entrepreneurs-best-branded-women.html.

11. Amy Jo Martin, "Give NASCAR a Chance," February 25, 2011, *Digital Royalty* (blog), www.amyjomartin.com/2011/give-nascar-a-chance.

CHAPTER 2: SMILE

1. "Could Moon Landings Have Been Faked? Some Think So," CNN, July 17, 2009, http://edition.cnn.com/2009/TECH/space/07/17/moon.landing.hoax.

2. "Landing a Man on the Moon: The Public's View," Gallup, July 20, 1999, www.gallup.com/poll/3712/landing-man-moon-publics-view.aspx.

3. Thomas Hargrove, "Third of Americans Suspect 9–11 Government Conspiracy," Scripps Howard News Service, August 1, 2006, www.scrippsnews.com/911poll.

4. "Social Values, Science, and Technology," European Commission, June 2005, http://ec.europa.eu/public_opinion/archives/ebs/ebs_225_report_en.pdf.

5. "Teeth Whitening," American Academy of Cosmetic Dentistry, www.aacd.com/index.php?module=cms&page=procedures/teethwhitening.asp&CTGTZO=-420&CTGTZL=-480.

6. "Charlie Bit My Finger—Again!" YouTube, www.youtube.com/watch?v=_OBlgSz8sSM.

7. "Hahaha," YouTube, www.youtube.com/watch?v=5P6UU6m3cqk.

8. "The Truth Behind the Smile and Other Myths: When Body Language Lies," Working Knowledge for Business Leaders (blog), Harvard Business School, September 30, 2002, http://hbswk.hbs.edu/archive/3123.html.

9. Nicholas A. Christakis and James H. Fowler, "Social Networks and Happiness," *Edge*, 2008, www.edge.org/3rd_culture/christakis_fowler08/christakis_fowler08_index.html.

10. Ibid.

11. "How Many Emails Are Sent Every Day?" About.com, http://email.about.com/od/emailtrivia/f/emails_per_day.htm.

12. Kit Eaton, "New Twitter Research: Happy Tweeting Could Win Business," *Fast Company*, March 16, 2011, www.fastcompany.com/1739325/attention-corporate-tweeters-be-happy-when-twittering-it-could-win-business.

13. Rosalind Picard, *Affective Computing* (Cambridge, MA: MIT Press, 2000).

14. Chris Brogan, "Emotions at a Distance," January 3, 2010, www.chrisbrogan.com/emotions-at-a-distance.

15. Wisdom Commons, www.wisdomcommons.org/wisbits/1274-a-smile-costs-nothing-but-gives.

CHAPTER 3: REIGN WITH NAMES

1. Rene Lynch, "The Pioneer Woman, an Internet and Publishing Sensation," *Los Angeles Times,* September 23, 2009, www.latimes.com/features/food/la-fo-pioneer23–2009sep23,0,623229.story.

2. "How Much Do Bloggers Make? Case Study: Ree Drummond AKA The Pioneer Woman," ABDPBT, www.abdpbt.com/personalfinance/how-much-do-bloggers-make-case-study-ree-drummond-aka-the-pioneer-woman.

3. Saddleback Leather, www.saddlebackleather.com/19-saddleback-story#bag.

4. From an interview with Dave Munson on April 18, 2011.

5. Saddleback Leather, www.saddlebackleather.com/19-saddleback-story#bag.

6. Ralph Waldo Emerson, *Letters and Social Aims* (Boston: James R. Osgood, 1876).

7. Nagesh Belludi, "The Art of Remembering Names," *Right Attitudes and Ideas for Impact,* www.rightattitudes.com/2007/12/11/the_art_of_remembering_names.

8. Nicholas Carr, "The Web Shatters Focus, Rewires Brains," *Wired,* May 24, 2010.

9. Roger Ebert, "The Quest for Frisson," *Chicago Sun-Times,* May 29, 2010, http://blogs.suntimes.com/ebert/2010/05/the_french_word_frisson_descri.html.

10. Information provided with permission by Dr. Howard Fine and J. D. Kuo, a brain tumor patient under his care.

CHAPTER 4: LISTEN LONGER

1. "Story," Dave Carroll Music, www.davecarrollmusic.com/ubg/story.

2. Ibid.

3. Chris Ayres, "Revenge Is Best Served Cold—on YouTube," *Times* (London), July 22, 2009, www.timesonline.co.uk/tol/comment/columnists/chris_ayres/article6722407.ece.

4. "Campaigns No Longer Matter: The Importance of Listening," Social Media Today, http://socialmediatoday.com/index.php?q=SMC/194763.

5. Ibid.

6. Clifton Fadiman and André Bernard, eds., *Bartlett's Book of Anecdotes* (New York: Little, Brown, 2000), 139.

7. Reprinted from original *How to Win Friends and Influence People* manuscript.

8. Shankar Vedantam, "Social Isolation Growing in U.S., Study Says," *Washington Post,* June 23, 2006, www.washingtonpost.com/wp-dyn/content/article/2006/06/22/AR2006062201763.html.

9. Ibid.

10. Jim Elliot and Elisabeth Elliot, *The Journals of Jim Elliot* (Old Tappan, NJ: Revell, 1978).

11. From an interview with the author. While the facts of the story are accurate, the subject asked to remain anonymous for personal reasons.

12. United offered Carroll belated compensation of $3,000; he had them donate it to a music-oriented charity.

CHAPTER 5: DISCUSS WHAT MATTERS TO THEM

1. Clifton Fadiman and André Bernard, eds., *Bartlett's Book of Anecdotes* (New York: Little, Brown, 2000), 489.

2. Ibid., 525.

3. Thanks to blogger Valeria Maltoni for her reference to the Doc Searls weblog from March 21, 2005, found here: http://doc-weblogs.com/2005/03/21#becauseCustomerRelationshipManagementIsAboutManagementMoreThanCustomers.

4. Valeria Maltoni, "Everyone Is Wrong About Influence," Conversation Agent (blog), July 7, 2010, www.conversationagent.com/2010/07/everyone-is-wrong-about-influence.html.

5. In an interview with the writer in January 2011.

6. Mitch Joel, "Making Sense of the Mess," Six Pixels of Separation (blog), March 8, 2011, www.twistimage.com/blog/archives/making-sense-of-the-mess.

7. As told to a former presidential speechwriter who was interviewed for this book.

8. Chris Gourlay, "OMG: Brains Can't Handle All Our Facebook Friends," *Times* (London), January 24, 2010, http://technology.timesonline.co.uk/tol/news/tech_and_web/the_web/article6999879.ece.

9. Joel, "Making Sense of the Mess."

CHAPTER 6: LEAVE OTHERS A LITTLE BETTER

1. In a series of interviews with the writer over the course of 2010 and 2011. Steve Scanlon's services and insights can be found at www .buildingchampions.com and www.realityandhope.com.

2. Caroline Wyatt, "Fans Hail Mona Lisa's New Setting," BBC, April 6, 2005, http://news.bbc.co.uk/2/hi/europe/4418425.stm.

3. In an interview with the writer on December 28, 2010.

4. David Brooks, "High-Five Nation," *New York Times,* September 15, 2009, www.nytimes.com/2009/09/15/opinion/15brooks .html?_r=2&ref=opinion.

5. Ibid.

6. Jesus, in the famous Sermon on the Mount, Matthew 7:12.

7. Richard Norton Smith, "Reagan Revelation: At 100, Why He Still Matters," *Time,* February 6, 2011, www.time.com/time/nation/ article/0,8599,2044565,00.html.

PART 3: HOW TO MERIT AND MAINTAIN OTHERS' TRUST

CHAPTER 1: AVOID ARGUMENTS

1. Nancy Gibbs and Michael Duffy, *The Preacher and the Presidents* (New York: Center Street, 2007), 46, 47, 48.

2. "Embattled BP Chief: I Want My Life Back," *Times* Online, May 31, 2010, http://business.timesonline.co.uk/tol/business/industry_sectors/ natural_resources/article7141137.ece.

3. Liz Robbins, "BP Chief Draws Outrage for Attending Yacht Race," *New York Times,* June 19, 2010.

4. "Lula, In His Own Words," *Time,* September 19, 2008, www.time. com/time/world/article/0,8599,1842949,00.html.

5. "Times Topics: Luiz Inácio Lula da Silva," *New York Times,* January 3, 2011, http://topics.nytimes.com/top/reference/timestopics/people/d/ luiz_inacio_lula_da_silva/index.html.

6. In an interview with the writer on March 25, 2011. Esther Jeles's insights and services can be found at www.ayletinc.com.

CHAPTER 2: NEVER SAY, "YOU'RE WRONG"

1. Deepak Malhotra, "Mistaking Mistrust for Greed: How to Solve the NFL Dispute," *Forbes,* March 14, 2011, http://www.forbes.com/2011/03/14/nfl-nhl-contracts-opinions-contributors-deepak-malhotra.html.

2. Wisdom Commons, http://www.wisdomcommons.org/virtue/56-friendliness/quotes.

3. In an interview with the writer on March 25, 2011. Esther Jeles's insights and services can be found at www.ayletinc.com.

4. Francis Collins, "Has the Revolution Arrived?" *Nature* 464, 674–75 (April 1, 2010), www.nature.com/nature/journal/v464/n7289/full/464674a.html.

5. J. Madeleine Nash, "Francis Collins: DNA Helmsman," *Time,* December 25, 2000, www.time.com/time/magazine/article/0,9171,998873,00.html.

CHAPTER 3: ADMIT FAULTS QUICKLY AND EMPHATICALLY

1. "Medical Aspects of Lightning," National Weather Service, www.weather.gov/om/lightning/medical.htm.

2. Mike Sunnucks, "PR Experts: Tiger Woods Could Lose Endorsements, Needs to Show Sincerity in Wake of Affairs," *Phoenix Business Journal,* December 2, 2009.

3. Ibid.

4. Richard Norton Smith, "The Reagan Revelation: At 100 Why He Still Matters," *Time,* February 7, 2011, www.time.com/time/nation/article/0,8599,2044565,00.html.

5. Chris Harry, "Jim Joyce, Armando Galarraga Real Sportsmen of the Year," AOL News, December 29, 2010, AOL News, www.aolnews.com/2010/12/29/jim-joyce-armando-galarraga-real-sportsmen-of-the-year.

CHAPTER 4: BEGIN IN A FRIENDLY WAY

1. John C. Maxwell, *The 21 Irrefutable Laws of Leadership* (Nashville: Thomas Nelson, 1999), 105, 106.

2. David Shaner, *The Seven Arts of Change* (New York: Union Square Press, 2010).

3. Sissela Bok, *Lying: Moral Choice in Public and Private Life* (New York: Pantheon, 1978), 26.

4. Shaner, *The Seven Arts of Change*.

5. Wisdom Commons, www.wisdomcommons.org/wisbits/2448-i-don-t-like-that-man-i-must.

6. Gary Vaynerchuk, "Building a Business in the 'Thank You' Economy," *Entrepreneur*, March 16, 2011, www.entrepreneur.com/article/219296.

7. Ibid.

8. The phrase is attributed to St. Basil the Great.

9. Vaynerchuk, "Building a Business."

CHAPTER 5: ACCESS AFFINITY

1. John C. Maxwell, *The 21 Irrefutable Laws of Leadership* (Nashville: Thomas Nelson, 1998).

2. Josh Bernoff and Ted Schadler, *Empowered* (Boston: Harvard Business School Press, 2010), 95.

3. Chris Brogan, "The Snowfall of Communication," February 4, 2011, http://www.chrisbrogan.com/thesnowfall.

CHAPTER 6: SURRENDER THE CREDIT

1. August Turak, "Giving Away Credit; Is It Worth It?" Forbes.com, November 8, 2010, http://blogs.forbes.com/augustturak/2010/11/08/giving-away-credit-is-it-worth-it.

2. Clifton Fadiman and André Bernard, eds., *Bartlett's Book of Anecdotes* (New York: Little, Brown, 2000), 545.

3. Richard Norton Smith, "The Reagan Revelation: At 100, Why He Still Matters," *Time*, February 7, 2011, www.time.com/time/nation/article/0,8599,2044565,00.html.

CHAPTER 7: ENGAGE WITH EMPATHY

1. Gerald Nirenberg, *Getting Through to People* (Engledwood Cliffs, NJ: Prentice Hall, 1963, p. 31).

CHAPTER 8: APPEAL TO NOBLE MOTIVES

1. John Eldredge, *Wild at Heart* (Nashville: Thomas Nelson, 2001), 18.

2. Amy Jo Martin, "The Business of Humanity," Digital Royalty (blog), www.thedigitalroyalty.com/2011/the-business-of-humanity. Reprinted with permission.

CHAPTER 9: SHARE YOUR JOURNEY

1. Jennifer Collins, "Making Cotton 'the Fabric of Our Lives,'" NPR, November 15, 2010, http://marketplace.publicradio.org/display/web/2010/11/15/pm making-cotton-the-fabric-of-our-lives.

2. Ibid.

3. Ibid.

4. Bob Brown, "Apple, Google Top Fortune's Most Admired Companies Ranking," Network World, March 3, 2011, www.networkworld.com/news/2011/030311-apple-google-admired-fortune.html.

5. "Buy One, Give One Free: TOMS Shoes," *Conversation Agent,* www.conversationagent.com/2011/03/buy-one-give-one-free-toms-shoes.html.

6. Amy Jo Martin, "Live Streaming. Ah, the Possibilities . . . ," Digital Royalty (blog), March 7, 2011, www.thedigitalroyalty.com/2011/live-streaming-ah-the-possibilities.

CHAPTER 10: THROW DOWN A CHALLENGE

1. Larry Bird and Earvin Johnson Jr., *When the Game Was Ours* (Boston: Houghton Mifflin Harcourt, 2009).

2. Proverbs 27:17.

3. Justin Levy, "Coca-Cola's Happiness Machine," January 20, 2011, http://justinrlevy.com/2010/01/20/coca-colas-happiness-machine.

4. Peter Lewis, "AOL vs. Microsoft: Now It's War," CNN Money, July 23, 2001, http://money.cnn.com/magazines/fortune/fortune_archive/2001/07/23/307401/index.htm.

5. Edmund Morris, *The Rise of Theodore Roosevelt* (New York: Random House, 2010), 32.

6. Ibid.

7. Ibid.

8. Tamara Audi, "Latest Prize in Celebrity Auctions Is a Tweet, Not a Meet-and-Greet," *Wall Street Journal,* September 23, 2010, http://online.wsj.com/article/SB10001424052748703860104575507581416301748.html?mod=wsj_share_twitter.

9. Amy Jo Martin, "TwitChange Takes Over Times Square," Digital Royalty (blog), January 21, 2011, www.thedigitalroyalty.com/2011/twitchange-takes-over-times-square.

PART 4: HOW TO LEAD CHANGE WITHOUT
RESISTANCE OR RESENTMENT

CHAPTER 1: BEGIN ON A POSITIVE NOTE

1. Max DePree, *Leadership Is an Art* (New York: Doubleday Business, 1989).

2. Sanjiv Ekbote, "Dale Carnegie Lesson 1: Begin with Praise and Honest Appreciation," *BookClub,* August 22, 2005, http://omnikron.typepad .com/bookclub/2005/08/sanjiv_ekbote_d.html.

3. Ray B. Williams, "Why We Love Bad News," PsychologyToday.com, December 30, 2010.

4. The study of impression formation has been popular since the 1950s. The focus on negative traits was once considered to be stronger than it is today, based on more recent studies, but even recent studies indicate that perceived negative behaviors or traits do affect impression formation more than positive ones do.

5. J. Sidney Shrauger and Saul E. Rosenberg, "Self-Esteem and the Effects of Success and Failure Feedback on Performance," *Journal of Personality* 38, 3 (1970): 404–17.

6. Trent Lorcher, "Leadership Principles for Teachers," Bright Hub, May 31, 2009, www.brighthub.com/education/k-12/articles/8881.aspx.

7. Robert Sutton, *Good Boss, Bad Boss* (New York: Business Plus, 2010), 235.

8. Sidney Rosen and Abraham Tesser, "On Reluctance to Communicate Undesirable Information: The MUM Effect," *Sociometry* 33, 3 (September 1970).

9. Robert Sutton, "The Mum Effect and Filtering in Organizations: The 'Shoot the Messenger' Problem," PsychologyToday.com, June 5, 2010.

10. Dale Carnegie and Associates, *The Leader in You* (New York: Pocket, 1995).

CHAPTER 2: ACKNOWLEDGE YOUR BAGGAGE

1. Marshall Goldsmith, *What Got You Here Won't Get You There* (New York: Hyperion, 2007), 85–86.

2. "Leaders Who Admit Mistakes Can Quickly Advance Their Careers," Institute for Health and Human Potential, May 21, 2010,

www.ihhp.com/speaking-coaching-training-blog/leadership-training/
leaders-admit-mistakes-quickly-advance-careers.

3. John Maxwell, *Failing Forward* (Nashville: Thomas Nelson, 2000), 52.

4. Portia Nelson, *There's a Hole in My Sidewalk* (New York: Atria Books, 1994).

5. Goldsmith, *What Got You Here*, 95.

CHAPTER 3: CALL OUT MISTAKES QUIETLY

1. *Los Angeles Times,* August 6, 1982.

2. John C. Maxwell, *The 21 Irrefutable Laws of Leadership* (Nashville: Thomas Nelson, 2007), 157–58.

3. Kerry Patterson, Joseph Grenny, David Maxfield, Ron McMillan, and Al Switzler, *Influencer* (New York: McGraw-Hill, 2008).

4. Ibid., 221.

CHAPTER 4: ASK QUESTIONS INSTEAD OF GIVING DIRECT ORDERS

1. D. Michael Abrashoff, *It's Your Ship* (New York: Business Plus, 2002), 44.

2. Ed Fuller, *You Can't Lead with Your Feet on the Desk: Building Relationships, Breaking Down Barriers, and Delivering Profits* (Hoboken, NJ: Wiley, 2011), 101.

3. Herbert H. Meyer, "Self-Appraisal of Job Performance," *Personnel Psychology* 33, 2 (June 1980).

CHAPTER 5: MITIGATE FAULT

1. Clifton Fadiman and André Bernard, eds., *Bartlett's Book of Anecdotes* (New York: Little, Brown, 2000), 123.

2. Robert Sutton, *Good Boss, Bad Boss* (New York: Business Plus, 2010), 77.

3. Fiona Lee, "The Fear Factor," *Harvard Business Review,* January 2001.

4. Brian O'Keefe, "Battle-Tested: From Soldier to Business Leader," *Fortune,* March 8, 2010.

5. Amy C. Edmondson, "Strategies for Learning from Failure," *Harvard Business Review,* April 2011.

6. Dale Carnegie and Associates, *The Leader in You* (New York: Pocket, 1995), 150.

CHAPTER 6: MAGNIFY IMPROVEMENT

1. "Chicago Hotel Combines Social Media and Employee Recognition," PR Web, August 5, 2010, www.prweb.com/releases/chicagohotel/socialmedia/prweb4347154.htm.

2. Gerald H. Graham, *Understanding Human Relations: The Individual, Organization, and Management* (Chicago: Science Research Associates, 1982).

3. Center for Management and Organization Effectiveness, "5 Ways to Give Praise: Small Efforts with a Huge Return," http://www.cmoe.com/blog/5-ways-to-give-praise-small-efforts-with-a-huge-return.htm.

4. D. Michael Abrashoff, *It's Your Ship* (New York: Business Plus, 2002), 142–43.

5. Timothy Evans, "The Tools of Encouragement," CYC-Online, International Child and Youth Care Network, Issue 73, February 2005, http://www.cyc-net.org/cyc-online/cycol-0205-encouragement.html.

6. Jon Carlson, L. Sperry, and D. Dinkmeyer, "Marriage Maintenance: How to Stay Healthy," *Topics in Family Counseling and Psychology* 1 (1992): 84–90.

CHAPTER 7: GIVE OTHERS A FINE REPUTATION TO LIVE UP TO

1. Rosamund Stone Zander and Benjamin Zander, *The Art of Possibility* (New York: Penguin, 2002), 27–28.

2. Ibid., 26.

CHAPTER 8: STAY CONNECTED ON COMMON GROUND

1. Kerry Patterson, Joseph Grenny, Ron McMillan, and Al Switzer, *Crucial Conversations* (New York: McGraw-Hill, 2002), 73.

2. Amy Jo Martin, "Celebrity Shares Phone Number with 4.3+ Million Fans," Digital Royalty (blog), August 30, 2010, www.thedigitalroyalty.com/2010/celebrity-shares-phone-number-with-4-3-million-fans-2.

3. Greg Ferenstein, "How Dana White Built a UFC Empire with Social Media," Mashable (blog), June 8, 2010, www.mashable.com/2010/06/08/dana-white-ufc-social-media.

4. Dr. Tim Irwin, "The Compass of a Leader," December 21, 2009, http://www.drtimirwin.com/newsletter-122109.html.

5. Yvon Chouinard, *Let My People Go Surfing* (New York: Penguin, 2005), 177–78.

6. Richard Branson, "Richard Branson on 'Social Relations,'" *Entrepreneur,* February 8, 2011, http://www.entrepreneur.com/article/218098.

ABOUT DALE CARNEGIE TRAINING®

Dale Carnegie partners with organizations to produce measurable business results by improving the performance of employees with emphasis on:

- leadership
- sales
- customer service

- presentations
- team member engagement
- process improvement

Recently identified by The Wall Street Journal as one of the top 25 high-performing franchises, Dale Carnegie Training programs are available in more than 25 languages throughout the entire United States and in more than 80 countries.

Dale Carnegie's corporate specialists work with individuals, groups and organizations to design solutions that unleash your employees' potential, enabling your organization to reach the next level of performance. Dale Carnegie Training offers public courses, seminars and workshops, as well as in-house customized training, corporate assessments, online reinforcements and one-on-one coaching.

 /dalecarnegietraining

 @DaleCarnegie

www.dalecarnegie.com

DALE CARNEGIE® TRAINING

More secrets to success from
DALE CARNEGIE

**HOW TO WIN FRIENDS AND INFLUENCE
PEOPLE IN THE DIGITAL AGE**
Available formats:
Hardcover, eBook, eAudio, CD

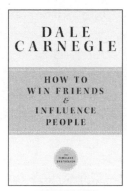

**HOW TO WIN FRIENDS
AND INFLUENCE PEOPLE**
Available formats:
Hardcover, Trade Paperback,
Mass Market, eBook, eAudio, CD

**HOW TO WIN FRIENDS AND INFLUENCE
PEOPLE FOR TEEN GIRLS**
Available formats:
Trade Paperback, eBook

**HOW TO DEVELOP SELF-CONFIDENCE
AND INFLUENCE PEOPLE BY PUBLIC
SPEAKING**
Available formats:
Mass Market

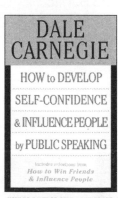

**HOW TO DEVELOP SELF-CONFIDENCE
AND INFLUENCE PEOPLE BY PUBLIC
SPEAKING**
Available formats:
Trade Paperback

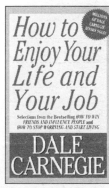

HOW TO ENJOY YOUR LIFE AND YOUR JOB
Available formats:
Mass Market, eBook, eAudio, CD